Contents

"Can't you smile just a little broader?" said the photographer.

"No, that's the best I can do," said Doc Prothro.
"I'm manager of the Phillies, you know."

HAROLD HELFER, *The Birmingham Post*, APRIL 10, 1939

SUMMER OF THE CHEAP WIENERS

What the 1941 Phillies Were Up To While Joe DiMaggio Was Making History

JUSTIN KLUGH

Havertown, Pennsylvania

Brookline Books is an imprint of Casemate Publishers

Published in the United States of America and Great Britain in 2026 by
BROOKLINE BOOKS
1950 Lawrence Road, Havertown, PA 19083, USA
and
47 Church Street, Barnsley, S70 2AS, UK

Paperback Edition: ISBN 978-1-955041-58-4
Digital Edition: ISBN 978-1-955041-59-1

A CIP record for this book is available from the British Library

Printed and bound in the United Kingdom by CPI Group (UK) Ltd, Croydon, CR0 4YY
Typeset in India by DiTech Publishing Services

For a complete list of Brookline Books titles, please contact:

CASEMATE PUBLISHERS (US)
Telephone (610) 853-9131
Fax (610) 853-9146
Email: casemate@casematepublishers.com
www.casematepublishers.com

CASEMATE PUBLISHERS (UK)
Telephone (0)1226 734350
Email: casemate@casemateuk.com
www.casemateuk.com

The Publisher's authorised representative in the EU for product safety is Authorised Rep Compliance Ltd., Ground Floor, 71 Lower Baggot Street, Dublin D02 P593, Ireland.
http://www.arccompliance.com

SUMMER OF THE CHEAP WIENERS

To my wonderful mom and dad.

Thank you for raising me to be kind
and for teaching me to love baseball.

Sorry for the cursing.

Preface

At the New York World's Fair in 1939, you could buy a hot dog for 10 cents and a tongue sandwich for 15.

Tongue was a chewy slab of pure, spongy muscle, the taste of which improved with the addition of watercress butter. It could be paired in a diner lunch special with an orangeade or a Budweiser and a cigar. Tongue *could* have been the mushy delight sought out by hungry baseball fans for generations, the organ connecting a nation's pastime to its stomachs.

Instead, we went for the wieners.

At an event called The Hot Dog of Tomorrow, there were 57 ways to prepare a wiener showcased, including one innovator with cheese and bacon. There were fried dogs. Boiled dogs. Broiled dogs. Steamed, cooked, and fricasseed.

"When a World Fair goes to all the trouble to publicize hot dogs and hamburgers you get some idea of the place of prominence they have come to occupy in our national life," noted one columnist.

Only a few years before, you would typically get a hot dog from the sleaziest booth at an amusement resort or off the back of a carnival wagon stuck in the mud.

"… you went for it only in moments when you didn't care what became of you socially," a writer explained.

It had already rivaled the peanut at ball games when President Franklin Delano Roosevelt announced he was a real wiener-hound and couldn't eat enough of them, boosting the hot dog's popularity. By the World's Fair in 1939, there were said to be 90 hot dog and hamburger stands cooking them different ways, and there would be three and a half of them sold for every attendee.

"Believe it or not, there are people who spend time figuring such things out," it was reported.[1]

When it wasn't waiting for the dogs to finish, America was going to the ballpark in the forties and people were going to need something to eat. With a classic era of baseball still in full swing, it would be accompanied by the wafting smell of sizzling wieners.

Hot dogs were the perfect concession item for the game, overlapping in both enjoyment and mystery: In their race to consume both baseball and hot dogs, fans had no idea what sort of future awaited either and had a few questions about what each was made of. By 1941, you'd be as likely to find a hot dog at the ballpark as you'd be to see Joe DiMaggio reach base, Ted Williams hit one in the corner, or the Philadelphia Phillies eat shit.

But the hot dog was more than just a totem of culinary invention that maybe had some rat meat in it. It was profits. Selling concessions was a big part of how team owners made their money, and they had an edible novelty to hock: Meat? In a *tube*?? Truly, this was a golden age of innovation as well.

Of course, they could only sell hot dogs to people if they came to their stadiums, and to get people to the stadium, you had to field a good team. There were plenty of good teams who could sell hot dogs in 1941. But there was also, at the bottom of the standings in both baseball and hot dog sales, the Phillies.

History that happened yesterday is easily recalled. But every time the sun goes down, it takes a little more history with it: Context. Detail. Less consequential happenstance that fills in the space between milestones. It all goes over the horizon and "history" consists of what remains.

The kinds of things Joe DiMaggio was doing in the summer of 1941 were the kind of things that remain. What the Phillies were doing was not.

But you know all about that. You know DiMaggio hit safely in 56 straight games. You know Ted Williams hit .400 for the season. You know that Pearl Harbor was, for the first eleven months of 1941, as obscure a naval base as it had been in 1940.

At this point in their history—which is to say, any time from the 1920s to the 1940s—the Phillies were known for their terrible, summer-long impressions of a baseball team. An influx of youth would periodically make the team look appealing and convince writers to do a story on how they might be turning a corner, until owner Gerald Nugent inevitably traded the Phillies' top talent for whoever was around or the nearest pile of money.

One such occasion was in 1921, when the Phillies went on a road trip and won five of eight games; a quite normal number of games for a team to win without anyone concluding anything of note. But since it was the Phillies, winning five of eight would be a sign of change, or perhaps from God; a harbinger of doom like when a bunch of birds break the silence by suddenly taking flight. Something was off, it seemed.

"The Phillies will have a strong ball club in the field in a very short time," Nugent's predecessor, William Baker, had claimed and expected to be believed. "I am determined to get together the best players available and give to the public the best brand of baseball."

These thoughts might sound strange from a man who had reportedly found the idea of his team winning five of eight so insane that he'd assumed reports of their latest victory in the paper had been a typographical error.[2]

The Phillies would lose hundreds and hundreds of baseball games from 1938 to 1942, at least 103 every year, and they wouldn't lose fewer than 80 games until 1949. They didn't hit, field, throw, or run well or consistently, and they certainly couldn't do more than one of those things at a time. They didn't build a lead and they didn't come back from a loss. They didn't even sell hot dogs, which meant they were starting to get the attention of the people who really mattered: rich people.

The Phillies, like many struggling 58-year-olds, had a roommate. To split the rent at Shibe Park, they shared it with the American League's Philadelphia Athletics. The A's were a franchise that hadn't finished with a winning record in eight years, but through their history, they had established a more dignified Philadelphia baseball standard under the brimmed hat and pensive glower of Connie Mack, for whom Shibe Park would one day be named.

The Athletics were outdrawing the Phillies, but everybody gets hungry no matter how good the home team is. There was nothing better to do when the Phillies were down 7-0 in the third than stretch the old legs with a walk down to the nearest wiener merchant. The 1941 Phillies were a poor lesson for anyone trying to introduce their child to the majesty of baseball, but at least they could introduce them to the majesty of hot dogs.

Sadly, attendance was so low at Shibe Park when the Phillies played that most of the concession stands were shuttered to avoid wasting money and resources when they could be used at other, better Shibe Park baseball games. The *Inquirer* had run a quote from St. Louis Browns manager Fred Haney the previous year in which he'd pointed out that only the ground floor restaurant and a stand on the second floor were typically kept open when the Phillies played—over 20 other precious revenue streams didn't even bother.

The paper was, at least, sympathetic to the working man: "The sales force, which works on a percentage and has to show up anyhow, usually has to suffer the added indignity of having to watch the Phillies' games."[3]

The *Camden Courier-Post* crunched the numbers and figured out that Nugent was getting to use Shibe Park for about $285 a game. Nugent stuck his nose in the air midway through the season and told reporters he had his pride, and his dignity, and his ball club, and despite his struggles to maintain all three at once, he would *not* be looking for handouts like some kind of unwashed hot dog-eater.

But uh.

He'd be *open* to charity, if anyone ... *felt like* offering it.

"Nobody's come forth to give us any help as yet, but I would welcome whatever comes my way," Nugent said, before adding, "I'm not asking for any."

"We've been through this thing before," he continued; a needless reminder that the Phillies were a longtime disgrace and not a sudden or unexpected one. "While it's tough, we're not giving up. No, sir, we're not giving up."

As the 1941 season approached, the Phillies were once again giving their fans a weak smile and a limp thumbs up. The city of Philadelphia sighed and found other things to do.

While this kind of season-long, citywide tragedy wasn't *new* for Philadelphia, it was starting to get *bigger*. The Phillies were now cutting into the *Athletics'* profits, so you might think the A's would respond with trash talk or legal action. Instead, they issued a statement full of something even worse:

Pity.

"We're sorry for the Phillies," the Athletics confessed, "and only wish we could do something to help them."[4]

Prologue

October 1, 1939

It poured in Brooklyn the day the Phillies became the worst.

Rain postponed several games on the last day of the 1939 regular season in Chicago, St. Louis, and Philadelphia. Fans hoping to catch some baseball at its most wet and meaningless were turned away at the gate and told to try again next season.

Before the 1939 season had gotten underway, writer Whitney Martin had gone down to spring training and polled fans on who had the best shot to win the National League (NL). Every team got at least a single vote. Except for one.

"The American League argument centers on the order of finish behind the Yankees, but the National League has its own little problem," Martin wrote. "It concerns the order of finish ahead of the Phillies, and it gets more answers than a telephone."[1]

Now, the season was wrapping up, and once more it did so with the Phillies squashed under the weight of the seven other National League teams on top of them. They headed up to New York and got swept by the Giants and Dodgers, picked up a single win in Boston, and then lost four straight to the Cardinals and Cubs. Something got into them during the final three stops of the road trip in Chicago, Pittsburgh, and Cincinnati, and they actually won three times in nine games, like some sort of sixth or even *fifth*-place squad.

But with their final losing streak of the season well underway, the Phillies lost 24 of the 30 games they'd played in September, finishing the month by getting swept in a doubleheader on the final day.

And then, for just a day, baseball's regular season dangled into October, momentarily delaying the vacations and reunions and winter shame spirals that awaited the sport's worst squad.

The Phillies were supposed to play two more in Brooklyn to end the season, but the rain had a schedule of its own and only permitted the Phillies and Dodgers to get in one. Kirby Higbe took the mound for the Phillies, hoping to squeeze out a win to make himself look better than the gutter trash with whom he shared a dugout.

Higbe wasn't overburdened with team spirit. He had been in no hurry to join the Phillies back in May, when he'd been traded from the Cubs. His new team was on its way to another 100-loss season, a fate to which they'd be chained by early September. Higbe's skipper in Chicago had apologized profusely for sending him to the Phillies, but apparently Higbe had been the only pitcher Phillies' manager Doc Prothro had wanted the Cubs to include in the deal for pitcher Claude Passeau.

A disgruntled Higbe packed his bags and reported to Shibe Park anyway, hoping every time he'd slip on his Phillies jersey and feel it cling to his flesh that it would be the last. It was like sending a man to the front of a stupid, poorly funded, and largely unnoticed war, in which the chief casualty was human dignity.

"When a good ballplayer went to the Phillies, he would hustle and bear down in the hope that he would be sold to a good ball club," Higbe explained in his autobiography. "It was hard to pitch for that club, but I kept thinking I would be with a good club if I kept on trying."[2]

Little had Higbe known, the Phillies *would* be playing baseball in October. Just not the kind anyone wanted, and a much worse kind than anyone realized.

The Phillies took a 2-1 lead in their last game of the season on October 1, giving Higbe a bounty of run support for once. Phillies infielder Emmet Mueller had connected on a home run in the top of the seventh that had given them the lead, meaning there were only nine more outs between the Phillies and a win that wouldn't send them to the playoffs or earn them home field advantage or even be witnessed by many people. It would simply be the more positive of the two potential outcomes. And with so close to nothing on the line, they could keep things loose and easy. No pressure.

They blew it immediately.

Higbe came back out for the bottom of the seventh and gave up a two-out triple to the Dodgers' Cookie Lavagetto. Higbe knew he couldn't rely on anyone behind him to save him. He'd have to pitch his own way out of trouble, knowing that he probably couldn't miss the bat of Dodgers hitter Dixie Walker, but he *could* get Walker to drive his pitch straight into the ground, at which point Higbe could field it himself and, hopefully, run it over to second without having to involve any of his lousy teammates.

With all the strength Higbe had left after a long, terrible season, and an additional seven innings in the rain—as well as all the desire within him to be on any other team in the world—Higbe unleashed his pitch and Walker's bat found it, smacking a grounder right at second base, a surefire out for anyone who'd been playing big-league baseball for more than a couple of minutes.

And as Lavagetto took off for home plate, the winning run closer with every step, the game was now in the quivering hands of Phillies second baseman Charlie Letchas.

Letchas had been a part of Doc Prothro's big plans in 1939. "The Phillies must be rebuilt from the ground up," Prothro had stated before purchasing the 23-year-old infielder from the Chattanooga Lookouts.

Letchas had been looking so unpromising earlier in the season that his Chattanooga manager had quietly brought in a new second baseman. But Letchas had warmed the hearts of all those watching with his "hustle, his grace in fielding his position, and his willingness to learn," and had eventually become part of the best double play combination in the Southern Association.

Prothro offering Letchas a deal was a wonderful conclusion to the kid's minor league success story. He was on his way to play for a major-league ball team! What a *shame* that it was the Phillies.

Nevertheless, Letchas was the one out there, waiting to receive Higbe's final out of the seventh on a rainy day when everyone was, in one way or another, ready for the end.

He dropped it.

The papers found different ways to describe what happened, but whatever it was, Letchas didn't look good doing it. The runner was safe at first, and even worse, Lavagetto was safe at home, and the Phillies' tight 2-1 lead was now a stupid 2-2 tie. Their lineup would only have two more chances to try to *un*tie it, and that would only be good news if they could hit. Which they could not. And Kirby Higbe knew it.

Higbe knew that worthless kid at second had been his only chance to get out of the inning, and more (most?) importantly, to impress any salvagers watching who were thinking of pulling Higbe off the Phillies' trash heap and giving him a shot with another, better club.

But that was all gone now, he felt, as the rain turned the dirt to mud. Higbe looked out at Letchas, threw his glove to the ground in anger, and took a second to stomp around the mound and yell at no one in particular.

Higbe couldn't blame Letchas, however, when he walked the next batter. And he couldn't blame the kid for Dodgers manager Leo Durocher swapping in a speedy pinch runner on second. And he couldn't blame Letchas for the next hitter knocking a single to right, *or* the throw from the Phillies' outfield being right on the money, but the Dodgers runner getting under the tag.[3]

The Dodgers went up 3-2 in the seventh and the Phillies went down 1-2-3 in the eighth and ninth. They lost the first game, the second game was washed out, and Higbe had to show up for spring training the next year, now a disgruntled member of the 19*40* Phillies as well.[4]

Losing was not a big deal for the Phillies.[5] From 1929 to 1941, it came as naturally as breathing. The Phillies and their incompetent American League counterparts, the St. Louis Browns, were known for nothing more. They were the two worst teams in either league, but since the dawn of America's Great Depression, the Browns had been the *worst* of the worst—until the Phillies made a late-era push to take the lead (in losing).

No one had likely realized it when Letchas had bungled a routine grounder and Higbe thought he had watched his future blundered away in the rain. But the Phillies had achieved something in their final error-driven defeat of the 1939 season: They had lost their 1,025th game since the start of 1929. Among teams' cumulative standings over the last

10 years, it put them a game *behind* the St. Louis Browns. And they never looked back. Or up, I guess.

The Phillies, from that day forward, would be the statistically worst team in baseball. Sixty-eight years later, they'd become the first American professional sports team to lose 10,000 games.

That same day, on October 1, 1939, Joe DiMaggio, the Yankee Clipper, won the American League batting title with a .381 batting average. Unlike in Philadelphia, you could catch a Yankees game and see players you'd actually heard of, who could hit and field, who *wanted* to be on the team they were on. Not even Hall of Famer Chuck Klein was on the Phillies anymore after they had released him in June, presumably out the back of a truck and into a field.

DiMaggio's status as an icon was underway. He was popular. He was incredible. He was baseball. He was hot dogs and firecrackers. He was going to have three daughters and name them Life, Liberty, and the Pursuit of Happiness. If these uppity Germans kept at it in Europe, they'd send Joe DiMaggio over there to deal with them. Or at least to Hawaii to sunbathe while someone else did.

DiMaggio was everything anyone wanted to see when they went to the ballpark by 1941 and his legend was only beginning. But there's always more to baseball than what's happening in the spotlight. For every tantalizing match-up, there was a quietly played matinee between fourth and fifth place squads earlier in the day. Seasons are remembered for their two or three most watched narratives, but there are countless stories told on every diamond. Sometimes the stories are quite boring. Sometimes they are very stupid. Sometimes they offer lessons; often, they offer nothing but a few quiet hours of a game some people love so much that they don't mind watching it played poorly.

On May 15, 1941, the Phillies had lost 19 of their first 27 games.[6]

They arrived in Cincinnati that day for a forgettable game against the Reds. Up in the Bronx, Joe DiMaggio knocked the lousy little single that would begin his historic hitting streak.

DiMaggio had been hitting .306 with five homers in the 1941 season's first four weeks. From May 15 to July 16, 1941, DiMaggio would hit safely in 56 consecutive baseball games.

From May 15 to July 16, 1941, the Philadelphia Phillies couldn't win more than two times in a row. The only thing lower than their batting averages were their city's expectations for their success. Nobody thought they were going to see anything out of Doc Prothro's boys. And as the summer went on, that was almost exactly what they got.

Are they important? No.

But are they *fun*?

Also no.

Let's begin.

Characters

In the box scores in which the 1941 Major League Baseball season played out, there were players now known as legends, stars, and studs: Joe DiMaggio. Ted Williams. Bob Feller. Pete Reiser. Johnny Mize. Arky Vaughan. Bobby Doerr. Bill Dickey. Joe Cronin. None of them played for the Phillies.

Here are a few of the names you'll see mentioned *ad nauseum* in the stories that follow.

Gerald Nugent, Team President

Nugent joined the Phillies as an assistant to the club president in 1926. After one year on the job, part of the Phillies' home ballpark at Broad and Huntington, the Baker Bowl, collapsed. Twenty-five people were injured and a man was trampled to death.

History has at times been gentle to Nugent, who some will tell you was more desirous of winning ball games than his predecessor but simply did not have the means. While some may focus on this more sympathetic portrayal, as the fans of the day felt, after a team has been losing as much as the Phillies had been for decades in 1941, it didn't matter what their team president's wants, wishes, or dreams were if he wasn't going to spend money on the team.

Nugent, identified as the club's "business manager," made it his business to point out that the stands had been inspected and "pronounced in good condition less than a fortnight ago."[1] Nugent and team president William Baker had been "interested spectators" at the court hearing that followed, in which they were cleared of responsibility in the fatal accident, which was said to have actually been caused by chronic heart disease.[2]

If a man's death wasn't enough to put Nugent off baseball, then he could stand working for the Phillies. And he'd do it using the baseball instincts and financial reserves he had obviously acquired in his previous career as a shoe salesman.

Phillies fans were tired of seeing them trade away good players for cash, as had essentially been company policy under team president William Baker. Baker had qualified for the position mostly by being the miserly, thoughtless, but fortunate cousin of his dead predecessor. When Nugent took over the Phillies, it was 1933, and the Phillies hadn't been particularly good, significant, or memorable since 1915, their first and only postseason appearance by that point.

Nugent was said to want a winning club, but given the limits on his resources, it wasn't long before he was smiling sheepishly and selling beloved players for cash and scraps just like Baker had always done. The 1941 season did not seem to be any different.

"The Phils got rid of Kirby Higbe, whose grand pitching couldn't balance the 100 grand Gerald Nugent could get for him," read one paper.[3]

It was a regular tradition for the Phillies to flip the script and win a couple of games, inspiring Nugent to pronounce that they were done selling their good young players and were ready to "start cashing in on 'em ourselves."

"Nugent's annual statements of fancy, however, are considered nice sentiment … but not taken seriously," read one paper. "It's doubtful if Nugent believes what he says himself."[4]

The Higbe deal specifically had earned Nugent the ire of commissioner Kenesaw Mountain Landis, who hadn't liked the shifty part in which the Phillies had also agreed to draft a specific player and then give him immediately to the Dodgers.

Landis launched an investigation, and though he ultimately found no wrongdoing, it only added to a busy winter for Nugent: When former Phillies second baseman F. Otto Knabe was arrested as part of a raid on a horse gambling den,[5] Nugent was one of several public figures who testified on behalf of Knabe's character.[6] Nugent's son broke his wrist, an injury Nugent had experienced himself twice as a youngster. His family adopted a five-week-old Irish terrier.[7] He attended the fifth annual reunion of the Reading Old-Timers club as a guest speaker. And he announced that the Phillies farm director would be resigning by the end of January and would be replaced by an empty chair.

"No one would be appointed to the post," Nugent told reporters, "because there was not enough work administering the Phils' farms to justify a full-time position."[8]

The post *had* been occupied by Jake Ogden, who was let go "probably for incompetency," theorized one writer who was so sure he was right and cared so little if he wasn't that he didn't even bother to confirm.

For a while, Ogden must have been Nugent's favorite person. He seems to have been doing a bunch of different jobs within the organization, and he found Nugent three of his best players—Nick Etten, Dan Litwhiler, and Tommy Hughes—for a collective $20,000.[9]

But there would always be more spots to fill; veteran third baseman Merrill May held out a bit as he and the Phillies argued over a $1,500 discrepancy in his contract, even though the whole time, May kept saying, "I'm not holding out" (he was). Alternatively, 36-year-old Phillies ticket-selling legend Chuck Klein was happy to fill a coach/pinch hitter/utility outfielder role.

But Nugent was content with his cheap, young, inexperienced, bad, cheap roster at the start of 1941, which became even more affordable when Phillies starting pitcher Hugh Mulcahy was the first big-league ballplayer drafted into World War II. Some executives would have jumped on their player like a grenade, futilely claiming the impact he'd have on the team here at home was more valuable than the difference he could make on the battlefield. But not Gerald Nugent.

"As far as the Philadelphia club is concerned, Mulcahy is in the army," Nugent said.

"And I'm glad to go," Mulcahy replied.[10]

Doc Prothro, Manager

Like all departments, the United States Army Dental Corps saw a surge of activity with the onset of World War I. Their rank and status were made equal to the more easily recalled Medical Corps, as hundreds of enlisted specialists made sure our boys were defending liberty with smiles that could light up a propaganda poster.[11] They also worked to prevent and address a litany of oral displeasures brought on by the horrific realities of war.

James Thompson Prothro was one of those boys, a limber Tennessean taking time off from his dental education for Uncle Sam.

"A clean-cut, easy-going fellow who could make friends anywhere," Prothro cut his postwar teeth on the baseball diamonds of Dyersburg, Tennessee, where all the players called him "Doc," but his wife kept things professional and called him "Thompson."[12]

As a semi-pro third baseman, he played a few games in front of a Washington Senators scout who'd been serving as an umpire. The scout wired his team that Prothro was worth a contract despite having "the shortest arms of any ball player in the country."[13]

On September 26, 1920, Prothro stepped into the batter's box at the Polo Grounds in New York. His playing days from 1920 to 1926 ended after 180 big-league games and a career .318 batting average. Prothro wavered between the majors and the minors until he was old, respected, and experienced enough to start serving as a player-manager, the first to request he fill such a role being Cubs owner Bill Veeck.

Red Sox owner Tom Yawkey brought in Prothro as part of his sudden attention to the Red Sox farm system in 1935, getting Doc to oversee his minor league team in Little Rock, where Prothro developed a reputation as a skilled manager of talent, youth, and ballplayers in general.

The Phillies signed him to manage their team in 1939, and by May of that year, his presence had already upgraded their projections from "last place" to "a very respectable last place."[14] Aging into a more boxlike, soft-bellied frame in his mid-40s, Prothro kept his ability to get a bang out of baseball, and his enthusiasm for the sport seemed to always find its way down to his players (at least until they started losing most of their games).

He was typically the coach in the third base box, as managers did at the time, striding in a six-pace radius and "chattering like a magpie." Prothro seemed to always be cooking something up so that the Phillies were only ever a double steal or the right pinch hitter away from potentially spoiling an afternoon for the other team. A lot of times, though, they fell short of even that, losing 106 and 103 games in 1939 and 1940, respectively. But even on his way out of town to go play for Leo Durocher and the Dodgers, self-loathing Phillies pitcher Kirby Higbe called Prothro "the best manager in the National League."[15]

As the 1941 season approached, Prothro was already getting the usual headaches. Nugent still owed him a second baseman. He would have 19 rookies to whip into shape in training camp.[16] Young stud outfielder Dan Litwhiler still needed to drop some weight.[17] The Giants were bugging Prothro about trading for Phillies shortstop Bobby Bragan or outfielder Joe Marty.[18]

One paper asked Prothro about the eight skippers hired to manage in the Southern League that summer, a circuit where Prothro had made a name for himself managing a team out of Little Rock, and one writer even theorized that he would have *preferred* to manage in Birmingham or Atlanta in 1941, had those Southern League teams asked him to before the Phillies' offer had come through.[19]

But Prothro was not one to wallow, though he did express regret in the spring of 1941 for not signing Dodgers shortstop Pee-Wee Reese to the Phillies when he'd had the chance to do so years before.[20] He was telling his friends that "all is well" with the Phillies by the end of March, around the same time his team capped off spring training with a five-error loss to the Reds.[21]

The Phillies' biggest problem, Prothro said, was actually four different problems: "too much dead wood, no spark, over-abundance of hams, and ingrown resignation to losing."[22] Despite these devastating issues and, apparently, a surplus of delicious hams, Prothro was unafraid to look the Phillies in the face for another season, earning him some momentary respect from the media.

"Put Doc Prothro down as a guy who can take it," said one writer. "He's signed again with the Phillies."[23]

Nick Etten, 1B

Etten was first spotted by a scout while playing for Villanova University, who ultimately decided to walk away without signing him. Years later, when that same scout saw Etten playing in the South Atlantic League as a 24-year-old, he felt serendipity was telling him to give the kid a shot and slipped Etten's name to Athletics manager Connie Mack. Presumably, something baseball-related also factored into his decision.

A hard slugger and a serviceable fielder, Etten was purchased by the Athletics in September 1938 after hitting .371 for Jacksonville in the Sally and contending for the league batting title. Mack, at the very least, needed a few dozen games of coverage at first base until his regular first baseman returned from injury. Etten joined "an army of rookies" meant to serve as reinforcements for the 1938 A's and Mack slotted him in as his clean-up hitter. Etten hit pretty well as long as they weren't throwing him curveballs.

A *Philadelphia Inquirer* comic at the time portrayed Etten, suitcase in hand, at a crossroads between two signs: "Join the Navy and see the world!" read one; "Play baseball and see the ball orchards of the U.S.A.," read the other.

"There's a career!" Etten was drawn to say, facing, naturally, the more whimsical and less life-threatening choice.

After the A's were done with him in 1939, it was back to the minors for a few years in Baltimore, where Etten struck extra base knock after extra base knock, hitting .300 and leading the International League with 126 RBI in 1940. Unlike many athletes before and after him, Etten dug into his Philadelphia-area stubbornness and seemed resolved not to leave the city.

"I am going to be around Philadelphia for a long time," he said in a letter to the Phillies in 1941, "so you might just as well get acquainted with me."

Bristling with confidence and new dad strength—he and his wife had just had a daughter—the 27-year-old Etten claimed he was in great shape after working out at the Skyline Athletic Club in Chicago all winter. The Phillies were convinced, cleared the expense with Nugent, and picked up Etten from Baltimore for a cool $10,000 to be their first baseman in 1941.

"You can't buy baby shoes with release slips, so Etten has his best foot poised," wrote Stan Baumgartner.[24]

Phillies coach Hans Lobert and first baseman Nick Etten. (Courtesy of the Boston Public Library, Leslie Jones Collection)

Tommy Hughes, Pitcher

Hughes, a 21-year-old right-hander, was notable for having to choose between signing with the Phillies or attending Duke University.

When asked in mid-May, as the Phillies approached their 20th loss in 30 games, whether or not he regretted the decision, Hughes told reporters, "Oh, I don't know." And if that wasn't bad enough, he *continued* speaking: "Sometimes I could kick myself in the pants for passing up a chance to go to Duke."[25]

Baseball is full of nonverbal thoughts with clear meaning: a head shake at a strike off the plate. A look back at the umpire. A rack of bats, thrown on the field. Only the least media-trained professionals would verbally and directly air a grievance in front of a microphone, especially one about their own team.

But 1941 was a different time for both the Phillies and the media, and there seemed to be a free pass for sliding on your Phillies jersey and saying, *"Damn, this sucks."* No one gasped or piled on. They simply nodded and hoped things would turn around for you soon.

Hughes had been a first baseman at Hanover Township High School in Pennsylvania, where the pitching had gotten so bad that his exasperated coach began letting position players start just to see if any of them could accidentally get an out. Hughes threw a two-hitter during his turn and was converted to a pitcher for the rest of his career.[26]

He trained himself by throwing through a tire, then a peach basket, then a six-inch hole in his garage. With one club as a minor leaguer, Hughes had a 1.83 ERA in nine starts and 85 strikeouts in 80 innings. He added some heat and a little control to his 1940 season in Baltimore, rocketing to the top of his manager's power rankings by throwing the first complete game of the Orioles' season. Tommy Thomas, the O's skipper, was often chuckled at because his eyes lit up whenever Hughes pitched, but in time, he'd be proven right: Hughes could put a twinkle in anybody's eye.

Of course, Hughes' critics had a few games to point to as well. On a cold day in 1940 when his teammates had been distracted by "keeping from freezing to death," Hughes was the frozen corpse responsible for an eight-run blow-up that turned an 11-3 victory into a 12-11 loss over the course of a single frostbitten inning.

Nevertheless, Hugh Trader, Jr. of the *Baltimore News Post* fell ass over tea kettle for the kid, calling him "the sensation of the International League" and "the richest piece of pitching property the Baltimore club has owned since Cliff Melton."[27] Trader saw the Orioles fetching at least $35,000 should they strike a deal with another team for young Hughes.

Such a price would typically turn Nugent and the Phillies away, but given their established working agreement with the Orioles, they technically had the right to acquire Hughes for a mere $10,000.

Actual talent on the cheap? Now they were speaking Gerald Nugent's language.

Hughes debuted for the Phillies on April 20, 1941. He pitched five shutout innings against the Giants but *officially* joined the team in the seventh, when a Bobby Bragan error allowed four runs to score and the Phillies lost, 7-0.

Bobby Bragan, SS

In addition to most other things, the 1940 Phillies needed some power in their lineup. "A consistent threat with a home run bat," Prothro fantasized that February when asked who else his team could use.

Any all-star solution to that need was met with a sharp look from Nugent and the sound of a checkbook slapping shut, so Prothro took an alternate route: cheap minor league options! Again!

Joe Marty, a .370 hitting outfielder from the Pacific Coast League, was his first choice. But Prothro also liked a certain "youngster from Pensacola" whom he called "my dark horse this year."

That would be Bragan, a middle infielder who had studied to be a minister but found more peace on the diamond.[28] He still needed to prove he could hang in the majors before anybody else would agree with Doc Prothro's scouting.[29] Bragan had been noticed in the minors over the years for dazzling defense and even a little scouting of his own; his Pensacola manager once signed a pitcher based on Bragan's recommendation.[30]

Bragan went on a tour of the south in the winter of 1940, visiting New Orleans and Birmingham and Pensacola, telling reporters he felt good and the reporters confirming that's how he looked, too.[31]

As the earth circled back around to spring, the Phillies still had a lot of jobs to work out. But Prothro was still high on his dark horse and told the 23-year-old Bragan to come to Phillies training camp in 1941 knowing that the shortstop job was all his.

Just don't look too good, kid, or Nugent will sell you to the circus.

"Dangerous" Dan Litwhiler, OF

What made Ringtown, Pennsylvania's Dan Litwhiler dangerous? Baseball was once a sport played by men gurgling tobacco juice in billowing jerseys who'd slap a rookie for cutting in line at batting practice.

Litwhiler, said to be "soft spoken, well-mannered and intelligent," represented a new era of gentleman ballplayers who could have a drink after the game without pissing themselves.

Despite what he lacked as a drinker and carouser, Litwhiler did lead the league in wholesomeness: His mother and his future wife made it to as many games as possible, while his blind father listened to Litwhiler's games on the radio. Once, when asked how she felt when Danny made a bad play, his wife replied that she didn't know; she'd never seen him make one.[32]

In four years of high school ball, his team only lost two games, and Litwhiler punched expectations even higher by homering in his first professional at-bat. He'd debuted for the Phillies at the end of 1940, hitting .345 in the season's last 36 games—Litwhiler, in fact, hit safely in 21 straight. Beat *that*, Joe DiMaggio!

Joe DiMaggio immediately beat that the following season in the stories you're about to read. But 21 is still a lot of games in a row to get a hit in the majors.

"The big difference is that everybody is much smarter," Litwhiler said about the difference between the major and minor leagues. "But that makes it all the more interesting."

"Interesting" was how Litwhiler's shoulder felt at the start of the 1941 season, as he learned more about the bodily cost of Major League Baseball. Which he likely understood: He'd only gotten his own chance in the bigs because the 1940 Phillies' outfield had been mowed down by an injury bug with a tommy gun.[33]

Fortunately, the check-ins with the Phillies' medical staff and a winter of doing construction work in Louisiana had left Litwhiler's arm and shoulder in tip-top shape for the coming season. People were expecting big things.[34]

A picture ran in the sports section of the *New York Daily News* on March 3 of Chuck Klein showing his bat grip to "Dangerous" Dan, characterizing theirs as a teacher-student relationship. Klein, an MVP and future Hall of Famer, was one of the better sources of hitting knowledge the Phillies had around to mentor their young sluggers. But how much help did they really need?[35]

"Klein hit .218 last year," the newspaper reminded us. "Litwhiler … finished 1940 with a batting average of .345."

Merrill "Pinky" May, 3B

On July 22, 1937, Joe DiMaggio entered play for the Yankees having hit safely in 22 straight games. The day ended without his 23rd. It was a little baby streak, a precursor to the monster he'd birth in the summer of '41. But the day his mini streak in 1937 ended, so did another one, way out in the Pacific Coast League.

Merrill May hadn't hit safely in nine straight games. He'd hit safely nine times in a *row*. Some would say this was a harder, cooler accomplishment than what DiMaggio had done, and others would simply say, "No it isn't; and also, who is Merrill May?"

May grounded into a double play in the fifth inning of a game to end the streak. "He came through with two bingles later on," lamented one writer, "but the thrill wasn't there."[36]

Nevertheless, one reporter stood up, finger in the air, and declared May's nine consecutive hits the longest such streak in Pacific Coast League history. Then, Lefty O'Doul, who had been out of professional baseball for three years, somehow heard about this, and made his own announcement: No, actually—it was *he* who had the longest number of consecutive hits in PCL history with 11 from July 16 to July 18, 1925.

O'Doul was vindicated, a storm of drama was stirred up among PCL scorekeepers, and Merrill May went on to play for the 1938 Newark Bears.[37]

The 1937 Newark Bears, a minor league affiliate of the Yankees, had plowed through the International League season with 109 wins and went 8-0 in the playoffs with a pair of four-game sweeps. Expectations coming into 1938 were, of course, that they would simply lumber through the league again like their namesake, ripping off car doors and feasting on the minor league competition cowering inside.

May, considered "an experienced infielder and a stout hitter," was, at 26, also a veteran of Double-A ball.[38] His defense at third had robbed countless hitters of extra bases down the line for years. A born Hoosier, he'd co-captained the 1932 Indiana University Bloomington squad to a Big Ten championship.[39]

The Bears' manager was right in his hesitation to compare the 1938 team with the 1937 squad. The '38 Bears won only 104 games and actually *lost* a few postseason games on their way to the championship title.

Still, they were deemed the best team in the league, and just as they had the last year, the Yankees applauded the Bears' success and then immediately began making the necessary phone calls to sell them all. The Yankees had Red Rolfe at third; they had no need for some capable third baseman in the minors like May hitting .333 … but someone else would. In late August, it was said that May "would be sold before the World Series."[40]

The Phillies had Pinky Whitney playing third and putting up fine numbers. But May, whose nickname was also "Pinky," was being eyed to replace him. May was drafted by Philadelphia, being considered the "prize" of the big-league draft meeting that year.[41]

His dream realized, May stepped to the plate in the majors at the geriatric age of 28. In his major-league debut with the Phillies, he pinch hit for Claude Passeau in the eighth inning and drew a pair of walks on the day, which ended in a 2-2 tie that the ump called early due to the sun going down.

May learned very quickly: On Philadelphia ball fields, the darkness is always closing in.

Si Johnson, Pitcher

The Reds were slated to play their minor league affiliate, the Rock Island Islanders, on July 31, 1933, and Rock Island had made an unorthodox request: Could the Reds please guarantee that one of their particular pitchers would get to pitch a few innings?

The Reds didn't have a guy the Islanders wanted to beat up on or a former legend Rock Island fans wanted to be able to say they saw. They *did* have Silas Johnson, a 26-year-old hurler who'd spent one magical season in Rock Island five years before.[42]

Johnson had made a name for himself by filling stat sheets with strikeouts on a semi-pro team out of Marseilles, Illinois. His 22-3 record and excellent command for a youngster was enough for Rock Island to hand him a contract.[43] The promising rookie was a "speedball artist" by the end of the season, saving his best performance for an early August start in which his fastball was unhittable except for a few ugly little tricklers that couldn't survive past the infield.[44]

"[Mississippi Valley League] President Belden Hill could have suspended half the Rock Island team yesterday, but as long as Silas Johnson was in the box, there wasn't a chance for the Islanders to lose," read the local Rock Island paper.[45]

A good fastball can get you some attention. But a great fastball can make a town fall in love with you.

As his career continued to take him over the hill to the next place, Johnson realized that you don't fall in love with *every* town. After leaving Rock Island, he was on his way to spring training in 1929 with the Reds in Florida by way of a train out of Chicago and had his luggage stolen at gunpoint. When he arrived in Florida with nothing, his teammates heard the story and started yelling "Stick 'em up, rookie!" at him.[46] Based on how rookies were treated by veterans at the time, Johnson was lucky his teammates ended the reenactment without shooting him.

By the time of the 1933 exhibition game back in Rock Island, Johnson had been a big leaguer for five years, but he hadn't forgotten that magical summer playing ball in that paradise on the Mississippi. He'd even shown up to a town hall meeting in Rock Island in 1931, when the Islanders had been threatening to shut down over a dispute with the league.[47]

The Reds received Rock Islanders' request to let Johnson pitch and responded with a charitable shrug. Their intensity level for the exhibition game was clear from moment one—their manager didn't even wear his uniform—and they let Johnson pitch for *eight* innings, to the delight of the Islander faithful. Johnson was only removed for a pinch hitter in the ninth because the Reds had started a six-run rally.[48]

In October 1939, Gerald Nugent paid $7,500 to acquire Johnson, but the Pirates wanted him so badly they offered the Phillies twice that to release him.[49] Doc Prothro figured if Pittsburgh wanted Johnson that badly, the Phillies might have fallen ass backwards into a hell of a pitcher. Why Nugent hesitated to make a profit in this particular case is unknown.

Johnson had spent six seasons with the Reds after leaving Rock Island, was traded to the Cardinals in 1936, and went up and down from the minors trying to get his aging arm to keep throwing fastballs. He was 33 years old when the Phillies brought him on board for the 1940 season and starting to gain the telltale gut of middle age.

Johnson was "round-faced" and "round-waisted" in 1939 spring training, about 10 pounds overweight and "having difficulty bending in the middle." Nothing, it was thought, that a little exercise in the hot Florida sun couldn't burn off.

Doc Prothro saw it, too, and introduced himself to Johnson by making him jog around the field to lose that winter weight. When Johnson and the two other players he was running with stopped for a breather, Prothro had them run another lap "just for the fun of it."[50]

"I like his spirit," Prothro said that year. "He's a great fellow around the ball club and if I pick his spots for him, I think he'll win a lot of ball games."[51]

But how *many* ball games was the question. Twelve, Prothro said, making sure to say he didn't expect Johnson to win 20 or even 15.

Expectations were locked in. By 1941, it was still taking Johnson a while to get back into playing shape, especially after being labeled "a big disappointment" the year before, but he was said to be in top form once again—and in the running to be the Phillies' opening day starter.[52]

But he never was much of a runner.

Johnny Rizzo, OF

Players with self-confidence can be a front office's worst nightmare. So many of us would rather appear humble, courteous, or unpretentious than tell someone we're worth more than what they're offering. Not Johnny Rizzo.

Rizzo wasn't afraid to walk into a room and pound his fist on a desk. In 1937, he did just that to get a better deal from the Pirates. And he did it with Joe DiMaggio's help.

The Pirates had needed an outfielder who could cover ground and hit hard. They'd found their man in Rizzo. They knew it. The fans knew it, too. So did the press. According to the first in a series of stories chronicling his rise to prominence in the organization entitled "The Rise of Rizzo," the 24-year-old Rizzo was reading his first contract with Pittsburgh in the winter of 1937 and didn't like what he saw. The figures were an insult—he was Johnny Rizzo, the next big baseball star—and he let the Pirates know it.

"You have heard of Joe DiMaggio of the American League," Rizzo wrote to Pittsburgh president William Benswanger. "I am going to be the Johnny Rizzo of the National League."

Maybe it was the fact that they were both Italian. Maybe it was that Pittsburgh had already deemed Rizzo worth giving up three players

Phillies outfielder Johnny Rizzo and an unknown player with some fans. (Photo courtesy of the SABR-Rucker Archive)

and a mountain of cash to acquire. Maybe it was simply invoking the DiMaggio name. But for whatever reason, that line made the Pirates up their offer to Rizzo, and he signed the next contract they sent him.[53]

Three years, a pedestrian slash line, and a terrible start to the 1940 season later, the Pirates tried to get as much "DiMaggio" out of the Johnny Rizzo deal as they could by trading Rizzo to the Reds for Joe's brother, Vince.

Rizzo was back with the Reds for a few weeks when they sent him to Philadelphia, and that was where he found himself at the start of the 1941 season: Still Johnny Rizzo. Still in the National League. Still not quite Joe DiMaggio.

Walter "Boom-Boom" Beck, Pitcher

Walter William Beck got his nickname by throwing a temper tantrum. Pitching for the Dodgers in 1933, he had his day ruined by the Phillies before he was even playing for them.

Everybody in a Phillies uniform came to play on July 4, 1934, and Beck only faced eight of them before the catcher came to take the ball away.

It's a humbling moment to be pulled in the first inning, the bases covered in the footprints of your shame. When they come to get you, you just take your butt pat and summon enough dignity to get off the field.

Or, you don't. It's your ball—at least until they take it from you. And they can't take it from you if you chuck it into the outfield.

So that's what Boom-Boom did. It was a hell of a throw—"the best fastball he has thrown this season," said one writer—and it smashed off the tin facade. The right fielder, naturally, had dozed off during the break while facing away from the infield. He was startled awake, assumed he was looking at a live ball, and jumped on it, throwing it into second.

And from that absolutely insane sequence, Walter William Beck got a nickname.

He also got released by the Dodgers that November.[54]

The Phillies had broken him, and from that moment forward, he began a sad, slow journey to join the league's most broken team, which was also the Phillies. In 1939, he reached them—reuniting with Doc Prothro, his manager when he played in Memphis—and stayed at the same level of "ineffective" for parts of five seasons, seeing less and less use as a starter.

Johnny Podgajny, Pitcher

At 20, Johnny Podgajny's quick delivery and tight command had made him an ace against Canadian-American League hitters.[55]

Phillies pitcher Johnny Podgajny, c. 1940–43. (*The Sporting News*)

A fine 1940 season for the Ottawa club got him the attention of the Philadelphia Phillies, whose attention was typically lamented or ignored. But a shot at the bigs is a shot at the bigs, and Podgajny was feeling a little bigger than the Class C leagues.

The Phillies dropped him straight into the majors, and though the lanky hotshot had been blasted out of his first start after a mere eight innings, he'd pitched all nine in his next three starts and only ever walked one batter. The Phillies even *won* one of Podgajny's appearances, which made him the starting pitcher for 2.3 percent of their win total for the season.

It took a skilled flinger to make the *Phillies* look better than shit and Podgajny had been that difference. He was sure of it. As sure as his name was Johnny Something.

It was pronounced puh-JONN-ee, if you ask his teammates, but Pod-GUY-neh if you'd asked his family. His parents were Polish immigrants, their Polish name confounding his teammates and flummoxing radio broadcasters.

Fortunately, Podgajny had glasses, so other players were legally required to give him the nickname "Specs." But when he came home to Chester,

Pennsylvania after the season, they just called him Johnny. Or maybe, "Johnny, that mad kid with the glasses."

He arrived back in Chester to a hero's welcome and spent that winter a head taller than everyone in town. Podgajny pulled some shifts at a Wilmington brickyard and regaled audiences with the story of his glory in the bigs. Soon, it would be spring again, and he'd head back to the majors, where—not sure if you've heard—he'd already found great success.

Spring did come. Podgajny did go back to the majors. And that summer of 1941, the nation was captivated by a ballplayer who became a model of consistent excellence.

That ballplayer was Joe DiMaggio.

Joe DiMaggio, Yankees Superstar

In March of 2023, the World Baseball Classic ended when Shohei Ohtani of Team Japan faced Mike Trout of Team USA: ninth inning, two outs, one-run game, Angels teammate vs. Angels teammate.

Ohtani struck out Trout, delivering the championship to Japan and capping off a WBC that had captivated the world with electric performances and exciting finishes throughout.

The next day on whatever show he was hosting, commentator Chris Russo lamented the stated epicness of the Trout-Ohtani showdown, bringing up Kirk Gibson's World Series homer from 1984 and claiming that Trout wasn't good because he "strikes out 175 times a season."

"Trout does nothing but strike out," Russo said as his guests slow blinked or covered their eyes in embarrassment. "Trout struck out twice in the game—and everybody talks to me about how Trout is DiMaggio!"

Trout struck out over 175 times in a season once, in 2014—the same year he led the league in runs scored, runs batted in, and total bases. The same year he was an all-star for the third of 11 times, a Silver Slugger winner for the third of nine times, and the American League MVP for the first of three times. And that's just of this writing. He may have won some more awards while I was typing.

The criticism of a generational player like Trout sounded bizarre or perhaps bait dangled for the ever-reliable rage merchants—until Russo got to DiMaggio's name. Then, it seemed clear what was going on: Somebody had compared Trout to DiMaggio once, Russo just wasn't having it, and the comment had lived in his head ever since.

Clearly, Russo felt that one of baseball's most universally famous figures needed to be defended in an argument that wasn't about him and that Russo himself had started. But that's simply how excited people can be to even mention Joe DiMaggio's name, even decades after his death: He's the measuring stick of baseball greatness, and some people like to beat you with it at every opportunity.

DiMaggio might be the most famous baseball player who ever lived. He made people fall in love with the game just by playing it in front of them. Some guys are just built to play baseball, and DiMaggio was the best one of those guys. His stats need not be stated to evoke his greatness; only his name.

But in the late '30s and early '40s, "Joltin' Joe" was still building the personal history to which people decades into the future would compare every great player for all time. And he hadn't quite reached "beloved" status yet.

As Americans were being asked to cut back in 1938, DiMaggio held out for $25,000 more on his contract. This was not viewed as particularly patriotic in exchange for "a couple of hours' exercise in the afternoon," and DiMaggio was booed as he came to the plate.

At 26 years old, he was lucky he was showing up for training camp in a Yankees uniform and not a U.S. military one. DiMaggio was getting a rep as an aloof, entitled figure, seemingly unaware or uncaring to the plight of the Average Joe who was working with a tiny household budget or getting notice to report to the draft board. But DiMaggio was literally an *above* average Joe, something he was about to make sure America knew from May 15 to July 16.

Leading up to that first hit of his historic streak, DiMaggio was once more being chided in the papers—not just for all the money he'd made as a ballplayer, advertising spokesman, and restaurant owner in a time when most of his countrymen could use a buck, but because he hadn't even been hitting that well.

In fact, compared with the Phillies' Hugh Mulcahy, who had answered Uncle Sam's call with a resounding and unequivocal, "Yes!" DiMaggio was looking pretty lame.

"What does Joe DiMaggio want?" one writer asked in the spring of 1941. "All the money and all the breaks!"[56]

DiMaggio had the nerve on May 15 to only be playing pretty well and not historically well for the Yankees. But he was about to embark on a nightly campaign to never go hitless again. In that time, DiMaggio was so locked in that he was playing a different sport than every player that would come before or after him.

Those players were mostly on the Philadelphia Phillies.

Part One: May

May 15

DiMaggio's first hit of his historic streak would have been quite pathetic and unextraordinary if not for the 90 other hits that followed. With two outs and Yankees shortstop Phil Rizzuto on second, he plunked a weak grounder to left and knocked in a run.

The Yankees lost, 13-1.

That same day, the Phillies had a day of *quite* uncommon feats: Not only did they pleasure their audience with Indiana University's 125-piece marching band before the game, but they managed to hit and field and keep their eyes from crossing long enough to win a ball game, 5-4.[1]

This was only one of 43 times they'd manage to win in a six-month span, so at this point in history, it's fair to say their actions on May 15 were more impressive than some slumping Yankee who managed to squeak one past the infield.

There were two types of players on the Phillies during this era of rampant bungling and fly ball misjudgment: those like Kirby Higbe, who went to work every day disgusted that it was a Phillies jersey draped on their bodies, touching their skin, stinging their flesh. And there were those who, on any other club, would never have gotten playing time, and were skipping to work each day because they played for the league's most welcoming team to below-average players.

Before the 1940 season, Higbe's luck changed. He was traded for a young catcher named Mickey Livingston, along with two other players, granting the tall, miserable starter his greatest wish: to no longer be in Philadelphia.

Livingston, a 26-year-old catcher who couldn't hit, was grateful for the opportunity to leave Brooklyn behind and take a train a hundred miles south into last place.

"The Dodgers' decision to send me to the Phillies was the best break I've ever had," Livingston told reporters, who presumably confirmed he understood how "standings" work. "Why, if I'd stayed up in Brooklyn, I'd have to break those other catchers' arms to get in a ball game."[2]

Livingston didn't have to go nuts on a teammate's forearm with a crowbar to get playing time anymore. He had come up competing with a few brash, mouthy young catchers who didn't mind scrapping with a heckler, but with the Phillies, Livington could remain his true self—calm, reserved, and probably staring down at the dirt instead of up in the stands for whoever was cursing at him.

With strategic beatings no longer a requirement to get in the lineup, Livingston wouldn't have to exchange prison time for playing time. Additionally, Higbe would no longer have to shiver with disdain each day he suited up. It was a rare trade that everybody won. Except the Phillies, who would lose 111 times.

Nevertheless, on the day DiMaggio's hit streak began, the Phillies were playing at Crosley Field in Cincinnati. Another former Dodger who'd come over in the Higbe trade, Bill Crouch and his "dinky curve"[3] lasted eight innings and held the Reds to three runs. This was typically more than enough to beat the Phillies, but on this day, they managed to yawn and stretch and bother to stir up a little offense with their coffee.

Nick Etten was always ready to be a hero, even if his glove wasn't. He'd been purchased by the Philadelphia Athletics in 1938 and repurchased by the Baltimore Orioles in 1939. With the O's, he joined an infield made up almost exclusively of ex-Athletics and impressed his new coaches by hitting with more power than he had ever had while pulling the ball with greater frequency. They did spot a few holes in his game, however, including "defense, and all things associated with it." Their attempted remedy for this included sitting him at first base and slapping ground balls at him for an hour at a time, swapping out batters about halfway through to ensure he wouldn't get lazy.

Etten improved enough with Baltimore that the Phillies decided to take advantage of their working agreement with the minor league squad and tap Etten for a promotion to the majors in 1941. By May 15, the 27-year-old first baseman was hitting .320 with a .944 OPS. The Phillies had a cheap slugger on their hands and could barely contain their excitement. Mostly about the cheap part.

With Etten in their lineup, the 2-0 and 3-1 deficits the Phillies wound up in at various points against the Reds were far less devastating. Etten came up in the top of the eighth with the Phillies down 2-0 and cracked a sac fly that halved the deficit. After the Reds added a third run to make it 3-1, the Phillies had one more inning to make something happen. Against all odds, what followed does in fact qualify as "something."

Two lead-off singles got the Phillies' rally started; a convenient number of base runners who, if knocked in, would tie the score. The pitcher's spot was up next, and nobody wanted to see Crouch hit, so Doc Prothro dispatched his happiest pinch hitter.

Livingston took in the moment. A successful sacrifice bunt had moved the two runners up to second and third. The Phillies had pulled off a precarious play and put themselves in a position to tie the game. Livingston approached the plate as everyone braced for an oblivious higher power to notice that the Phillies were actually in a good spot and fire a lightning bolt at Cincinnati.

Instead, he put the bat on the ball and sent it rocketing into the right-field grass, bringing both runs in and tying the game at 3-3.

Phillies third baseman Merrill May added an RBI single and Etten came back up and blasted *another* sac fly that brought in an insurance run to make it 5-3. Runs? Leads? *Insurance* runs? Just who did these Phillies think they were, the Dodgers? Up in Brooklyn, the nose hairs began tingling inside Kirby Higbe's nostrils as the team he so passionately loathed began doing something that wasn't entirely loathsome.

But the Phillies needed to keep their new lead intact for three more outs—which offered a lifetime of opportunities for the Reds' lineup. Cincinnati's second baseman, Lonny Frey, had been particularly annoying all day, hitting an RBI single in the third that had opened the scoring. The Phillies had then showed who they were, attempting to pick him off, failing, throwing the ball into the stands, and allowing Frey to reach second base as they tried to negotiate to get the ball back. Frey was due back up in the ninth, and now that the Phillies had pulled their starter, it'd be up to reliever Ike Pearson to close things out.

Pearson had been the ace starter at Ole Miss, and after being signed by the Phillies in 1939, stories of his exploits in the mystic commonwealth of Pennsylvania were routinely churned through the headlines of his home state as Mississippi waited for their local boy to make good.

"The Mississippi Madcap," Stan Baumgartner once called him. Pearson would play in five non-consecutive seasons of big-league ball, broken up by a few years of shooting at people for Uncle Sam. The 1941 season would be his best, and at the end of it, he'd be the National League leader in games finished *and* in hitting people with the baseball. No wonder Uncle Sam scooped him up; he'd been taking target practice for months.

In late April, Pearson would hit the Dodgers' Pete Reiser in the face but didn't have the velocity to break any bones. People were generally content to sit there and watch the Phillies waste their own time, but when they started dragging other, more promising players into their shame-spirals, it was frowned upon. So, a month after the incident, Reiser hit a grand slam off Pearson and it was viewed as righting a wrong. It might have sent more of a message to Pearson had Reiser hit a grand slam into his face, but that probably would have been tough to talk even Pete Reiser into.

Pearson entered the game for the Phillies in the ninth with a 5-3 lead, courtesy of Etten and Livingston. He got a strikeout and a ground-out to start the frame, inching closer to elusive victory when the Reds snuck in a pinch hitter: Jimmy Ripple. Ripple doubled to right, putting a runner in scoring position for the day's most irritating Reds hitter, Lonny Frey.

Frey had been "tickled"[4] to go from the Cubs to the Reds in 1938, as the move would mean an increase in playing time and he was said to have improved on defense, having recently been taught how to turn a double play. He was always considered a solid player with class but never got further than the verge of breaking out. In 1940, he was held back from an exhibition game in Havana, Cuba, due to a heel injury that some players might have played through. His manager at the time, however, had explained that Frey just wasn't "the rugged type."

Frey might not have been rugged and was continuously described as a "little guy" (he was five-foot-ten, 160 pounds), but he was leading the 1941 Reds in RBI by the end of April. Collectively, the team's offense wasn't on fire, but Frey had been reliably productive, and he looked to add another RBI to his total as he faced Pearson in the ninth. He blooped a looper[5] into center, letting Ripple come around to score, and cutting the lead to 5-4.

So, there was Reds shortstop Eddie Joost, with the tying run on base and two outs. At this moment, Joost was but a modest infielder with a California smile who held the major-league record at the time for single-game chances at shortstop, having successfully fielded 19 out of 20 ground balls. But in time, Joost would get to know Philadelphia well.

Years later in 1948, he'd be playing shortstop for the A's when a grounder would get past the pitcher. Ranging to his right to field it, Joost would put his glove down and the ball would disappear. Everyone was waiting for him to make the throw, but the runners reached first and third safely as the A's pitcher ran over to Joost, flailing his arms, screaming about where the ball was.

It had somehow bounced off the heel of Joost's mitt, rolled up his sleeve, and disappeared into his jersey. After scrambling around like his skin was on fire, Joost managed to find the ball, but at that point, the play had burned up. The runner who'd reached third, one of Joost's personal heroes, was laughing his ass off.

"It was definitely the most embarrassing moment of my life," Joost would recall. "And the worst of it was that Ted Williams was laughing his head off at me. I looked like a real dunce."[6]

The biggest humiliations were still ahead. For now, the Cincy shortstop suffered a more normal one. Pearson got Joost to whiff at his last pitch, and the Phillies won, 5-4.

Up in the Bronx, Joe DiMaggio had a real shit day. He had two hits stolen from him—a grounder deflected off one fielder to another, and a line drive speared out of the air. He also hit a guy in the back with a throw. If it hadn't been for his RBI single—his first hit in three days, the

New York Daily News noted—the Yankees wouldn't have scored at all as the White Sox beat the crap out of them, 13-1, for their fifth straight loss.

When the 1941 season is viewed, it's remembered only for its epic milestones and for that reason, is considered a historic and important year in baseball. But in this single-day snapshot, we are told a different story: That the Phillies could use strategy, competence, and just enough offense to win a close ball game. That Mickey Livingston was a clutch hitter. And that New York was starting to wonder after three long, hitless days, when was this DiMaggio kid going to get his shit together?[7]

"When Joe DiMaggio singled home Phil Rizzuto in the first inning of the Yankee-White Sox game on May 15, it was his first run batted in with a hit since May 1," read one report. "That may have had some bearing on why the New Yorks had trouble."[8]

May 16–17

A shadow of evil was cast across the European continent. British forces beat back the Nazis in West Egypt, German troops were reported to be moving through France and its colonies, and the United States was muttering that it may start having the Navy protect its interests in the Red Sea to ward off Axis interference.[1]

Each day, the world inched closer to catastrophe until, in mid-May, the unimaginable finally happened: The New York Yankees lost five games in a row.

By May 16, 1941, the Yankees had to be considering disbanding, especially when it looked like the White Sox would give them their sixth straight loss. New York scored four runs pretty quickly, but Chicago ripped apart their pitching in the sixth and took a 5-4 lead. The Yankees sat quietly in their dugout, considering their future careers as waiters and door-to-door salesmen.

But then, something magical happened: The Yankees started hitting, almost as though it was the 1940s and they were the New York Yankees. DiMaggio led off the ninth with a triple and was knocked in by another triple to tie the game at 5-5. The White Sox intentionally walked the next two hitters to load the bases with no outs on purpose, their plan working perfectly as moments later Yankees pinch hitter Red Ruffing knocked a single to left that won the game.

The victory would end the Yankees' longest losing streak of the season. They would never lose more than four in a row again. In the end, they decided not to disband.

DiMaggio's triple, and his home run earlier in the game, were noted as having broken him out of a "terrific slump," as he hadn't hit a homer since April 27 and it had been two entire days since he'd had three multi-hit games in a row.[2] Truly desperate times for the Bronx Bombers. They'd gone through the trauma of having to live with a little less for a few days, but it was time to play like a 101-win team again.

The Phillies may not have had a lot of good players, but they did have a couple of them, and a few others it was hoped could be good some day in the future.

Of course, there were good players on *other* teams, and there was a practice at the time, as well as today, in which teams *could*, in theory, acquire players from other teams in exchange for some of their own players. This was called "trading," and still is. The Phillies may or may not have been aware of this.

Another flurry of trades had just rocked the league, and a bunch of players were in different uniforms, each team believing they had gotten the better of the other. It was jarring. Upsetting. Baseball at its most heartless. Children woke up to learn their favorite players had left town, probably forever. But the Phillies had not received a phone call, nor had they apparently made one … at least not one with an appealing enough trade offer coming through the line.

"The Phillies are shunned, while the rich in the majors go around preparing to get richer," said one writer. "What have the Phillies done to deserve [this]? Seriously, what have they done?"[3]

Why would no one trade with the Phillies just because none of their players were desirable? It was downright un-American. A time had come in which the Phillies were a team for which few players sought to play, few fans went to see, and with whom no teams wished to trade.

The Dodgers had made deals, the Cardinals had made deals, the Giants had made deals. The Phillies, with their okay-ish-at-best players compared to the rest of the league, could have used a trade or two to at least shake things up. But, that same writer eventually concluded, there was a pretty clear and obvious reason for this.

"The Cards and the Giants are good clubs, unlike the Phillies," he wrote, "who merely are a club."

They were a club with a day off on May 16, and Phillies players and fans were having a great old time. Not just because they were having a day away from last place, reveling in the victory they had secured over the World Series champion Cincinnati Reds the day before.

It had been the Phillies' fourth straight win over the Reds, making them undefeated against the champs so far in 1941. They would go on to play each other 18 more times throughout the season. The Phillies would win twice.

But they lived in blessed ignorance of the future at this point. And on their off day it was said that the Phillies were having themselves a laugh at the Reds, the so-called defending champions of the world, who now apparently had fallen so far that they couldn't even beat the *Phillies*. And the Phillies, said the Phillies, were *terrible*.

"The Phillies today were chuckling over the plight of the champions and gloating over the fact that they have helped greatly in making them appear to be chumps instead of champs by winning all three games they have played with them," read one newspaper.[4]

The Reds seemed to agree with the Phillies. Having only won three of their last 13 games as they slumped in chunks in front of their home fans, there were some serious changes coming. Losing six games in a row was one thing, but losing four games to the Phillies came with a deeper level of shame; a shame typically felt exclusively by the Phillies. One columnist suggested the only appropriate punishment for the Reds' underachieving players was "a sentence to the Phillies, or some minor league whistlestop."[5]

The Phillies weren't the kind of team that could typically humiliate and laugh at another one. The kind of team that could was their Shibe Park roommates, the American League's Athletics, piloted by Connie Mack. The tall, pensive baseball lifer had the respect of everyone in the sport.

Mack was 78 years old in 1941, but still 15 years from his death. He had long ago entered the part of his career in which his accomplishments were being converted into trophies and plaques, and chances were good that if you bumped into him on the street somewhere he was likely on his way to be honored for something.

May 17 was Connie Mack Day in Philadelphia, so in this case, what he was being honored for was being Connie Mack. His 40-year stewardship of the Athletics was admired by fans and teams across the league for assembling a pair of dynasties that won a total of nine American League pennants and five World Series titles.

The home run was not a nightly event in baseball when Connie Mack was coming up as a player in the late 1800s. Watching homers go over the fence was like watching rockets blast off into space. In Mack's first year as a player for the 1886 Washington Nationals, there were 413 home runs hit in the entire league.

In 1941, the Yankees alone hit 151. Joe DiMaggio blasted one of them off the A's as Mack stood there and watched, probably less entranced by a ball going that far than he'd been decades before.

"Connie Mack, who learned his baseball in the days when a home run was a rarity, became more familiar with the glorified fourmaster here today," wrote one columnist.[6]

The Phillies were fortunate. With the A's in the other circuit, they only had to play them in exhibition games. In 1941, the Athletics would occasionally squint at the Phillies with unstated concern, seeming to wonder if it was more helpful to aid them or let them bleed out.

But there was no envy between Mack and Phillies president Gerald Nugent, at least none that Mack would air publicly. He referred to Nugent as an old friend of his in his memoirs, mentioning how the two of them, as well as Pittsburgh Pirates president William Benswanger, had been early financial supporters of American Legion ball in Pennsylvania. And on May 17, Connie Mack Day at Shibe Park, Nugent was going to hand his pal Mack an award.

As Nugent's Phillies beat the Reds and got dangerously close to their 10th win of the season's first 30 games, Nugent helped present Mack with the Citizens' Plaque. The two of them were pictured among others on the front page of the *Philadelphia Inquirer*, each looking at a different photographer.

And while rainstorms lurking in the area scared off a lot of the fans, they still managed to honor Mack in a celebration that had been conceived and suggested by one of his neighbors. He had an original song written for and sung to him, music from the police band, gifts from fans, players, and umpires, as well as speeches, including one from Nugent, who credited Mack for giving him hope not just for baseball, but all mankind.

"Mr. Mack," Nugent said, "anything I might say here would fall short of expressing how the fans of America feel toward you. You belong to the people of this country. All your innate modesty fails to conceal a life symbolic of good, inspiring deeds past and present and for the future. It is men like you who stabilize our faith in human nature."[7]

Nugent would never have as honorable or successful or acclaimed a career as his contemporary Mack. He was the current spot-filler in the role of Philadelphia Phillies president, and while he was from the city and had been a Phillies fan growing up, his background as a shoe salesman left him limited financially if rich in team spirit. Teams can benefit from a desire to win, but they rarely accept it as payment.

As a player in the late 1880s, Mack played in the National League for about 10 years and hit five home runs. That meant he technically had achieved more personal success in the National League than Nugent had as the team president of the Phillies, despite Mack exclusively running an American League team for the last 40 years.

That's why Connie Mack had a day named after him and Nugent had a pitcher who was publicly regretting choosing the Phillies over going to college.

"If things work out all right this season," Tommy Hughes said, "I might be able to go to college in the fall and take some extra night work."[8]

A legend like Mack could inspire hope in anyone. As Nugent handed Mack his plaque on Connie Mack Day, he hoped his team would win some more games in '41, that people might eventually remember that there were *two* ball teams in Philadelphia, and that maybe someday he'd be standing on the field, waiting for someone to hand him a plaque with *his* name on it.

Of course, the Phillies were technically renting Shibe Park from the A's at the time. So while Mack might have been an inspiring friend to Nugent, in a less inspiring way, Nugent was about to hand an award to his landlord, to whom he would be two years behind in rent by the end of the season.

May 18

The *Philadelphia Inquirer* had a question for its city on May 18: "*What is wrong with our world?*" Understanding that no one person can answer that question, they smartly expanded it to four people: a socialist, a social worker, an educator, and a public official, all of whom seemed to orbit the same three points:

No one wants to fight for what they believe.

No one can see past their own prejudices.

No one is willing to face reality.

The paper made it clear it wasn't looking for *solutions* to these problems, just to gather an idea of what the problems *were*. Each person gave expanded responses based on their perspectives, and readers nodded in agreement or sadly shook their heads; careful, of course, to not count themselves as a part of the "No one" incriminated by each bullet point.

Meanwhile, 200 local school children picked up trash and scrubbed every surface in Germantown as part of a two-month cleanliness campaign. They left signs around the neighborhood for the residents to see the following morning that read, "Please Keep This Lot Clean." It was a task that seemed to deny each individual point raised by the socialist, social worker, educator, and public official, as the kids fought for a cleaner city by facing the reality that they were better off cleaning it themselves.

The Phillies, too, had more reality to face, and on May 18, that reality was flying in from St. Louis.

Cardinals catcher Walker Cooper had started the year hot, hitting .357 by early May. His skipper, Billy Southworth, had seen something special in Cooper during spring training, undoubtedly smiling and nodding in the background while watching Cooper interact with the pitching staff and mature into a fine young ballplayer. The previous year, Cooper had been a stubborn rookie who'd gotten into a bit of a rhubarb with an umpire. Afterward, he'd learned that if you want to stay in the game, the best thing to say to an umpire is nothing. He'd never really have an issue with one again.

A player like that can have limitless value for a manager; a player that he can rely on to handle the lollygaggers, to be his right hand, to run the clubhouse as a respected peer of the players, rather than the authority figure who decides if they get to play or not. In 1941, Cooper's bat had cooled off after April and he had slumped through his last 19 at-bats. But Southworth knew Cooper's leadership skills and determination were part of why the Cardinals had started 20-8. He was more valuable than anything he did at the plate, Southworth knew. To an extent.

But then Southworth watched in slow motion as Cooper smashed into Phillies second baseman Harry Marnie. The manager's favorite son was obliterated. Cooper's dislocated collarbone and general shoulder crappiness was said to sideline him "indefinitely," and he wouldn't be back on the field for almost two months.[1]

It was a hell of a price to pay for a game against the Phillies.

The Phillies, as a team, were respected in the league only slightly more than the equipment. Playing them had an expected, and frequent, outcome. But there were the Phillies on May 18, leading the Cardinals 4-1 and standing over the body of Billy Southworth's right-hand man. Tragically for Doc Prothro and his team, there were still four innings left. And revenge only takes one pitch.

The Phillies had been getting no-hit for five innings by Cardinals ace Morton Cooper until they stacked up four runs in the sixth. This break in Cooper's dominance may have had something to do with him watching his brother, Walker, get wrecked on the infield and leave the field in horrible pain.

The Cardinals responded with one run per inning until the end of the game. Lee Grissom had made the start for the Phillies, a Texan stricken with left-handedness at an early age. He had appeared on the Phillies roster earlier that month. The Phillies apparently had soured on lefty reliever Vito Tamulis, acquired as part of the Kirby Higbe trade, and, in desperate need of an inexperienced arm with command problems, had swapped Tamulis back to the Dodgers in exchange for Grissom.

Three years prior, Grissom had appeared in the back of a comic book, the June issue of *Action Comics*, along with Babe Ruth, Lou Gehrig, and Sam Leslie as sports stars of the day. Having grown up near the banks of the Red River, Grissom would never be as famous as the superhero with which he'd shared a comic book, but like Superman, he did once punch a man so hard that he died—though Superman likely never faced a lot of manslaughter charges the way Grissom did, ultimately being acquitted.

Also like Superman, Grissom occasionally had to do everything himself. On May 18 while pitching for the Phillies, he had started to labor by the seventh inning, likely even more gassed from having to knock in his own insurance runs. But the Cardinals just kept smacking singles off him and suddenly Grissom was going out to protect a 5-4 lead in the ninth.

He got the first out, loaded the bases, took a breath, got his mind right, believed in himself, felt space and time align, went into his delivery, and gave up a walk-off single for a Cardinals win.

Another Phillies win streak, or at least win pair, was snapped. The Cardinals got the win even though they lost their team leader in Cooper, who was said to have suffered a fractured shoulder that would keep him off the field for two months. Suddenly, St. Louis had a need for a catcher—they were scuffling with the Dodgers for control of the standings and couldn't step in a bucket this early in the fight. Whoever Cooper's replacement would be, he'd have to come from nearby.[2]

No team was closer than the one that had cost Southworth his first catcher. Rumors of a potential trade going down between the Cardinals and Phillies before the Phillies left for Chicago started being whispered in St. Louis; at first breathily, then aggressively.[3]

Ass-backwards into the lap of fate they fell. Could this be it? The Phillies' big trade? Finally, having done nothing but blasted the other team's catcher to pieces, they had an opportunity to acquire a *new* player! They hadn't had a trade market, so they had created one, and all it had taken was another man's entire wellbeing. Nevertheless, the Phillies showed up at the Cardinals' door hours later to offer them a deal for a *new* catcher without a hint of shame. Create demand, become supply.

The Phillies front office didn't want to talk about it. The Cardinals didn't want to talk about it. And Doc Prothro didn't want to talk about it. He was angrily pounding soda in his office, wondering if he'd ever get some pitchers who could at least point to the strike zone on a map.

Besides, there was another game tomorrow for Prothro to think about. He was going to try to squeeze the Phillies' third win in four games out of some poor matchups: The Phillies were starting Tommy Hughes, his head full of regrets, against a Cardinals starter who'd thrown a one-hitter only two weeks prior. Was the one-hitter against the Phillies? Obviously, yes.

It was becoming clear, and likely had been for some time: Prothro didn't have a Joe DiMaggio in his lineup.

Up at Yankee Stadium, DiMaggio popped out in the fourth inning, but the umps probably said, "*That's okay, Joe; you can go on down to first base anyway.*" They cleared him of the out on account of catcher interference, DiMaggio went to first, and the call led to the Yankees mounting a four-run rally. DiMaggio had already gotten his hit for the day out of the way with a first inning single. Now they were just giving him a victory lap.

Of course, as the Phillies knew better than anybody: Two hits aren't a streak, just like two wins aren't a streak—just a pair of happy accidents. Even a team with only 43 wins could do something *twice*. If Joe DiMaggio wanted everybody's attention, he'd have to get a few more hits than two in a row. And if the Phillies had wanted everybody's attention, they should have had a Joe DiMaggio. Though they would have settled for Superman.

In 2011, the *Action Comics* comic book with Lee Grissom's face in it sold for over two million dollars. This is largely credited to it featuring Superman's first appearance and not Lee Grissom.[4]

May 19–20

"The uncertainty of baseball is its chief lure," read one paper in May 1941. "You can never tell what'll happen next." Then, quoting Detroit Tigers owner Frank J. Navin: "If those things didn't happen, we'd have to close every ballpark in America."[1]

Like all things, the ambiguity of baseball is often overstated. Yes, you don't know *exactly* what is coming on a nightly basis, but you have a general idea of who is going to hit the ball where; how a starter is going to pitch; what a manager will do in a situation. Baseball is an attempt by humans to control chaos as its intensity is gently dialed up over nine frames. The statistics it generates are meant to pinpoint potential future outcomes, and now modern baseball is all about predicting the future in order to try to control that, as well.

The specifics aren't just always unknown; they are unknowable. But when we start talking about baseball like it's a big sexy mystery every night, what we're talking about are bad hops and bloop hits. You generally *do* know what's going to happen next: The pitcher is going to pitch. The batter is going to react.

The ball will be in the mitt or in the air or on the ground.

It was early in the season, but the Phillies had already proven that they were becoming one of baseball's pillars of consistency: Not every night, but *any* night, the 1941 Phillies were going to lose.

In 1941, people weren't being drawn to major-league ballparks for the suspenseful dinner theater and chest-clutching cliffhangers. They weren't actually coming at all.

"Whether you know it or not, this is one of the strangest and most disturbing big-league baseball seasons yet," wrote Cy Peterson in the *Philadelphia Inquirer*.

Peterson had two reasons for labeling 1941 such a bizarre disaster:

1. Teams that were typically good were now bad.
2. Fans weren't coming out to watch as many games.

Indeed, the sun had risen on May 20 and daylight had crept across some curious National League standings—much different than they'd been a year ago. The Reds had tumbled far out of the top spot, the Dodgers and Cardinals were both 20-game winners much earlier in the season, and even the Phillies were already *in* last place instead of spiraling toward it.

So yes, executives were all about marketing the sport as an unsolvable summer riddle in which anything could happen and nothing was ever the same. But in truth, the second things shifted in a way no fans had seen before, baseball was naturally considered broken beyond repair.

When the upper tiers of baseball aren't making money—or even just not as much money as before—it's *everybody's* problem. At least, they'll tell you it is. Today, the move is to get into a bitter dispute with the city over a new stadium and threaten to leave town forever. The worst ones will actually do it, too, even if their relationship with the city is so bad that they wind up having to play a few years in a minor-league stadium somewhere else. It's one of those things that everyone generally agrees is bad but no one who thinks so can stop it.

But in 1941, the solution for owners not getting as good a gate take as they had in previous years was to start playing in the dark.

Connie Mack and Gerald Nugent were part of a group of executives who believed Americans were just too goddamn *industrious* in the daytime and were less inclined to bring their "pockets full of boom cash" to the ballpark when they were still on the clock.

One glance around Shibe Park on a typical weekday would be enough to convince someone that baseball wasn't drawing in Philadelphia, and one glance at the team on the field would likely be enough to explain why. But when the people failed to pack Shibe Park for *Connie Mack* Day, everybody knew there was a bigger problem.

It definitely wasn't the price of a ticket, the *Inquirer* assured its readers, which was up to $1.14. It was the fact that people couldn't afford to leave a $15–20 an hour job just to watch their home team's latest ass-kicking.

By moving games to the *evening*, the owners could squeeze some cash out of these working stiffs by getting them to use their remaining energy to traipse down to Shibe Park, buy a hot dog, and watch the Phillies get their asses kicked. And then maybe buy a second hot dog.

Other evening-based sports like boxing or midget car racing were said to be selling out their events, proving that it could work for baseball. But laborers who worked early mornings and had their afternoons free were economically cajoled into picking up second jobs to fill their time, rather than spending more money watching a team stay in last place.

Baseball, it seemed, would address its owners' concerns by moving into the twilight hours. While a couple franchises appeared to be hold-outs, ballparks with proper lighting could see half of their remaining schedules switched to night games.

With that problem solved, there was still the other one: "… instead of the expected league balance," Peterman wrote, "1941 thus far has brought an excess of sloppy clubs."[2]

A grim picture of the Phillies' chances was painted, with their hopes at a World Series berth only possible following a purely theoretical and near-impossible series of what-ifs. But c'mon! It's baseball! Anything can happen! Remember?!

When the Phillies were away, Shibe Park switched to an American League ballpark. The Athletics were having some pitching troubles, too, but were clearly a superior, or at least closer to mediocre, team than the Phillies. And even so, there were always cooler, better teams than the Phillies stopping by Shibe Park with players on their roster people actually wanted to see, so there was always a reason to catch a game!

Reminded once more that they were killing baseball, the Phillies took the field in St. Louis for another poorly attended matinee while the rest of America *worked* for a living.

The most certain outcome, a Phillies loss, appeared to be the most inevitable as well, as the Cardinals took a 4-0 lead into the sixth. Phillies starter old Si Johnson just didn't have his fastball again, which was an outcome as certain as any other. Cardinals first baseman Johnny Mize repeatedly ate Johnson's lunch, knocking three extra-base hits on the day and driving in all four St. Louis runs.

But then, instead of giving up, the Phillies didn't. They were facing a struggling starter in Clyde Shoun, who had taken the loss in his last two games and had an ERA approaching 7.00 but still shut down the Phillies' lineup through the first six innings. Armed with a four-run lead, Shoun entered an uncharacteristic state of skill and focus, or at least appeared to, as he was pitching against a team with neither.

Also predictable was that the Phillies' chances of winning the game improved immediately upon Si Johnson's removal from it. His pinch hitter, George Jumonville, had knocked in a hundred runs for Ottawa the previous year, and was up with the big club to provide a little power. He crushed a solo shot to put the Phillies on the board in the sixth, and in the eighth, they tied it at 4-4 on a Nick Etten double before walking it off in the eleventh. They had 16 hits on the day.[3]

The anomalous power surge probably left onlookers stunned. But elsewhere, such prowess at the plate was not so strange to see. From May to July of 1941, DiMaggio logging a hit was the closest thing to a certainty baseball had ever seen. And the longer people could rely on it, the more interesting it became, because this was baseball, and there is no greater draw than a challenge to its uncertainty.

Unless that challenge was the Phillies, a team as certain to lose a game as DiMaggio was to log a hit during it. But over the course of the summer, under the lights, even the Phillies, it seemed, could surprise you.

May 21

Joe DiMaggio said he decided to hit more home runs in 1941 right after hitting a really long, really satisfying home run, three days into the season. It was off Nels Potter of the Athletics, it went 460 feet, and he hit it in the ninth inning, though tragically it was a solo shot when the Yankees were down by four.

He did say that he went to the plate every time after that looking to put the fear of God into the ball. From spring training and for eight games into the regular season, DiMaggio had a hit in 27 straight games using his new "homers only" philosophy. But as with every player before and after him with the same mindset, it ruined his swing and wrecked his approach.

Then, on April 22, DiMaggio went 0-for-Tuesday against Les McCrabb and the Philadelphia A's, and thus had begun the worst slump of his career. Audiences and writers could only clutch their heads and watch as their hero's season batting average dropped below .300 for the first time anybody could remember. That wasn't just a ballplayer having a bad stretch. That was a *Yankee* mired in a slump. That was two-time American League batting champion *Joe DiMaggio* flailing around and walking dejectedly back to the dugout. That was *America* hitting .135 over its next 52 at-bats.

Hell, for the last month of the 1940 season, DiMaggio had suffered from a bruise on the base of his thumb that had impacted his swing so much that all he had been able to do was lift the bat to meet the ball, and his batting average *still* went up 10 points. Therefore, the only thing that could save him from his current slump was the longest hit streak of all time. Also, shortening his grip and "concentrating on meeting the ball" helped. But DiMaggio wasn't going to slump forever—he wasn't *Mike Trout*, after all.

The adjustment, it seemed, had paid off. DiMaggio was hitting again, and he wouldn't stop hitting until mid-July, but nobody knew that yet.

They just knew that tighter swing was paying off. Sure, he wasn't slugging moonshots onto the street, but he was cracking line drives all over the field. As even DiMaggio pointed out, he'd hit a bunch of clean line drives on a recent road trip and almost all of them had been outs, but that didn't mean he wasn't hitting the ball.

"I never hit a ball better in my life than one that was turned into a double play ball in Cleveland," DiMaggio said.[1]

So even his *slumps* were well-executed at this point. If DiMaggio could see positives in poor outcomes, certainly the Phillies could—

Let me stop you right there. The Phillies had hit into very few outs that could be considered moral victories; typically, the outs *they* made just meant they had to get off the field.

A wire service broke down May 21's baseball action listing the most impressive individual performances of the day. It also listed the goats, those fools who'd stepped on the diamond expecting anything other than humiliation.

Top to bottom, they'd found the worst of the slate and put all their names in print. Not only that, but the list also included an epitaph explaining each player's inclusion, as though it were an obituary for the dignity of each. And there, at the bottom of the casualties, read the demise of the Phillies' starter:

"Frank Hoerst, Phillies; routed by Cubs."[2]

Hoerst had made it five innings into the Cubs' batting order. His nemesis of the day was Bill Nicholson, the Cubs' right fielder whose unhappiness in life was said to come from ever having to face a left-handed pitcher. Surely Frank "Lefty" Hoerst, who was recovering from breaking his leg while playing basketball over the winter, would win the day.[3]

With the Phillies up 3-0, Nicholson faced Hoerst in the fifth with the bases loaded. Moments before, he'd watched his third baseman, Merrill May, throw a sure double play ball home to catch a runner streaking for the plate. The ensuing rundown ended with Phillies catcher Bennie Warren failing to tag the runner before he retreated safely to third, and then Warren getting ejected for some "saucy talk" at the umpire regarding the call.[4]

Warren had gotten a dirt shower earlier in the evening when a slow roller to first base had ended in a play at the plate. The umpire had called that runner safe, too, and the Phillies catcher was sick of hearing calls he didn't like.

So Hoerst may have been a little rattled with the lead gone—the Cubs had tied things up at 2-2—and Chicago's most monstrous slugger stepping in. His best defense against Nicholson was being left-handed, something that seemed to flummox Nicholson about any hurler.

Until now. Nicholson parked a grand slam to deliver the Cubs a 7-3 victory.

Hoerst's routed body was dragged off the field.

May 22–24

It was May 23, and the Phillies were in last place, trapped beneath every other NL team with a 73-run differential on top of them. They were, however, still a baseball team, as one sports columnist noted. This was an accomplishment, he wrote. At least symmetrically: "After all, the National League has to have eight clubs."

But these words were not written to congratulate the Phillies for "hanging in there" or something. Instead, they pointed out once again that no matter how deeply the Phillies were buried beneath the National League basement, the year would be a success for Gerald Nugent, because he had players to sell.

The Phillies were being called out. Occasionally this would happen in letters to the editor or passing comments in the press or the grumbled and shouted complaints as fans took in a ball game at Shibe Park. But every so often, all of the letters and comments and grumblings were gathered into a pile and published as a column to remind the world that the Phillies were still terrible and they hadn't come up with a better plan than gutting their roster and seeing who was around to fill it back up.

It's not like they weren't good at what they were doing. The Phillies were able to grab promising young players, presumably once they were out of earshot of anyone who could have warned them about the Phillies. Then, the team waited to see if their new stud would become worth anything more and, in time, sell him to whoever they could. It's a business model that has delighted owners and bummed out fans for generations.

And the Phillies were nailing it. Five of their young pitchers were catching eyes across the league: Gordon Pixley, Frank Melton, Johnny Podgajny, Tommy Hughes, and Frank Hoerst. Hughes had an offer from

Boston for $40,000, but his minor league team had a working agreement with the Phillies, which meant he had to stay in Philadelphia, where he'd been acquired for a quarter of that. The Dodgers had used the Phillies as a puppet to draft Melton, with the understanding that the Phillies would use their pick to take the kid, then swap him to Brooklyn for a price, but the commissioner found out about it and shut that backroom deal down. Now the Phillies just had a guy around who everyone, including the Phillies, had expected to be on the Dodgers by now.

Both of the Phillies' catchers, Bennie Warren and Mickey Livingston, were said to be of interest elsewhere, too. Plus there was young slugger and defending International League RBI leader Nick Etten at first, and even George Jumonville, the recently promoted pinch hitter who'd smacked a game-saving dinger the other day, got a shout-out.

With this many promising players, you'd think the Phillies would have had a more promising team. But the roster was largely anonymous to national audiences. As one writer put it, "They're like a dog's tail—they may cover plenty of ground but they are always last!"[1]

Nothing says "promising" like being compared to the ass of a dog. This was the other half of the argument submitted a week prior; yes, the Phillies had sat out trade season. But they were happy to make *deals*. Trades were moves that swapped out a good player for a good player at a position of need. Deals were moves that saw a useful player swapped out for several less or not-at-all useful players and typically some sweet, sweet cash. Deals also included rationalizations for the move, as though each sell-off was just a convincing explanation away from the fans being on board.

But for the Phillies, "worse" was the expectation. When other franchises sunk that low, people looked up from their breakfasts. When the Phillies did it, they just kept reading the paper.

For a while in 1941, it had been the Reds whose losing was causing concern. But now it was the Dodgers' turn, losing six straight, including some heartbreakers against the Reds. Brooklyn was out of pity for anyone but themselves—a sentiment their local paper described as classlessly as possible.

"Today [the Dodgers] have no sympathy to spare for the inmates of a Hitler concentration camp," wrote Tommy Holmes in the *Brooklyn Eagle*.[2]

The good news, for the Dodgers anyway, was that their upcoming schedule softened a bit as they prepped for five games in Philly ("patent medicine, guaranteed to cure slumps," playing the Phillies was said to be).[3] There were even 2,000 Dodgers fans coming down by bus for a pep rally, and Philadelphian baseball fans were so beaten down and disinterested that they would let that sort of thing happen without an appropriately violent response.[4]

The Phillies had their second game against the Cubs postponed due to rain so they were coming home after a not particularly invigorating 7-3 loss. By game time against the Dodgers on May 24, they hadn't played ball since May 21. This meant that for almost three complete days, they hadn't lost a game! And yet, in that beautiful space untainted by defeat or embarrassment, tragedy had wedged its way in.

Former Phillies catcher Jack Clements had been born near 19th and Lombard and started his playing career as an outlaw with the Union Association. He was a teenager when the Phillies brought him in to play on their 1884 squad, and despite being tragically born left-handed, Clements was a catcher for 16 years in the big leagues, including 14 at least partial seasons with the Phillies. Nobody caught that much for the Phillies again until Darren Daulton in 1996.

Clements was a round-headed, square-shaped, hard-swinger who could park one over the wall, same as his teammates Sam Thompson and Ed Delahanty. Some say he was the first catcher to wear a chest protector that wasn't his own sternum.[5] When the Phillies' manager, Harry Wright, went blind, Clements handled in-game decisions for 19 games, a bold move for Clements after he'd seen Wright suffer the impact of watching the Phillies too long.[6]

Clements had died on May 23, 1941, in Norristown; ringless, pennant-less, and 76 years old. Not even a chest protector can save you from a heart condition, and in the end that's what got him, ending his life with Clements having only witnessed one Phillies postseason appearance in the three-quarters of a century he spent on earth.

A known and beloved player's death always served as an unfortunate reminder for how long the Phillies' pump-and-dump (only with no pumping) roster scheme had been going on. The Yankees had a full history of icons whose passings would be announced for periods of national mourning. But when the Phillies lost a favored, distinct, and highly skilled player from their own history, they likely had to remind anyone from out of town who he was.[7]

Along with Sam Thompson and Ed Delahanty, Clements had made a habit of sending baseballs to heaven over the right-field wall at Broad and Huntingdon.

"He did not seem to be handicapped by being a left-handed thrower for a catcher," read the *Inquirer* upon Clements' death, staggered by his ability to thrive despite his left-handedness.

As they mourned a member of the Phillies family, the Phillies could've used even just a moment of triumph into which to channel their grief, and fortunately, their first game against the Dodgers provided it. Kirby Higbe was on the mound, glad to be far enough from the Phillies so as not to get their stink on him, and eager to show that he was better than the team on which he'd played the year before. He would go on to lead the league in walks and earned runs—all in a Brooklyn uniform.

Regardless, Higbe was ready to win on May 24. The Phillies stumbled after a 2-1 Dodgers lead until the eighth inning, when finally, Nick Etten made something happen. With a man on, he took Higbe deep and gave the Phillies their first lead of the day, 3-2, and it was up to Tommy Hughes to protect the one-run lead for six outs.

The Phillies deserved a moment to feel good. It passed quickly. Hughes went out to pitch the bottom of the inning and would allow seven hitters to come to the plate between the second and third outs. The Dodgers would score five times, snap their losing streak with a 7-3 win, and get excited about playing four more games against the Phillies.

Everybody was streaking that Saturday. Just not always in the same direction. Joe DiMaggio's Yankees had just won three in a row, meaning all was right in the universe once more.

A *Daily News* photographer caught DiMaggio as he over-considered second base and raced back to first with a sprawling slide: arm extended, legs stretched in opposite directions, the first base coach frantically pointing in the foreground, and the first baseman with an outreached mitt waiting for the ball to arrive just a second or two late. Together, they almost looked like some kind of malformed baseball horror with limbs and hats protruding from every side. Instead, it was something much easier to believe: Joe DiMaggio reaching base safely.[8]

With the 6-5 win over Detroit, the Yankees crawled over the Red Sox into third place in the American League. After a 9-9 tie with the Red Sox, they came back the next day to win, 7-6. DiMaggio's arm was looking better from the outfield and he'd have plenty of balls to retrieve, given the Yankees' pitching struggles.

His hit streak now on to 10 games, his defense on the mend, and the Yankees on fire, DiMaggio was emerging as baseball's biggest monster, and he was doing it without any extra limbs.

The real monsters were of course the Phillies, who were rampaging from town to town, losing every game they could find. But there's too much baseball to lose the whole summer, and the Phillies' next win was only four losses away.

May 25–28

The Phillies didn't make a lot of friends in 1941. Sure, a lot of people stopped by, but their unique combination of "cheap" and "incompetent" turned off their fans, other team's fans, writers who covered the team, and owners with meat wagons full of hot dogs to sell.

Throughout the summer, there were plenty of times in which the Phillies were discussed in harsh whispers and angry shouts about the detriment they were to the rest of the league. DiMaggio, at least, didn't make fans feel stupid for watching baseball.

But as league races became clear, suddenly the Phillies were a more valuable commodity.

The Dodgers "need the Phillies like ham needs eggs," editor Jimmy Wood wrote in the *Brooklyn Eagle*, celebrating the Dodgers' victory over the Phillies in game one of a five-game set.[1]

When NL teams wanted to sell tickets, the Phillies were the enemy. But when they wanted to tighten up a playoff race? Well, well, well; look who suddenly wants to play a team that sucks.

Even Doc Prothro, who was the manager of the Phillies, wasn't going to get caught on the record advocating for the Phillies. When the *Brooklyn Eagle* interviewed him, they were staggered by his gushing proclamation that the Dodgers were the best that the National League had to offer—and the American League, too.

"Prothro has no dream of illusions about his club and because that is so, it's doubly fruitful to chin with him," the paper read.

As all action movies have taught us, there's no man more dangerous than one with nothing to lose. It was late May, and in baseball, Doc Prothro was already that man.

"He doesn't have anything else to bother him except developing some interesting talent like Kirby Higbe and peddling them off for a fair price while Gerry Nugent nods amiably," the paper continued. "That being the case, when he sounds off, it isn't to gratify an inflated ego. He really means it, brother."[2]

Prothro said he felt the Dodgers could beat anybody in the Senior Circuit, and with their mix of youth and experience, they could probably handle the Junior Circuit, too. He felt like the Cardinals' new studs, like Hank Gornicki and Johnny Grodzicki and Sam Nahem, would melt in the St. Louis heat. He said the Reds had "no punch" and an "overrated" pitching staff. No one said the name "DiMaggio" even once.

He didn't seem to have anything to say about the Phillies, but the love-struck *Brooklyn Eagle* writers, dazzled by Prothro's ability to compliment a team beyond his own very bad one, didn't really want to hear about them anyway. They wanted to hear him say how talented and deep the Dodgers were, and how he'd be securing a seat for the World Series in Flatbush, which he said on his way out of the room.

"If the Phillies will keep on losing to the Dodgers," read the paper, "we're sure he means it."[3]

It wasn't an exaggeration that the Dodgers needed the Phillies. Against them and the second-to-last-place Braves by May 26, the Dodgers were a combined 11-0. Against every other opponent, they were 13-12. The Phillies (and Braves) were the reason(s) Brooklyn was at the top of the league.

And the Phillies continued being that reason for the Dodgers, who were fueled by a sadistic need to crush defenseless weaklings, and when they played the Phillies, revenge.

Brooklyn outfielder Pete Reiser is famous for being as good as Willie Mays (according to Leo Durocher), and for being incredibly injury prone because he could only play at the highest level of intensity. Reiser threw himself into walls with such frequency that he left the field on a stretcher more times than anyone else in baseball history to that point. He fractured his skull running into a wall once and played with a broken arm for weeks before getting an X-ray. There's a reason he is credited with making the Dodgers relevant in Brooklyn. There is also a reason he retired early, which was that everything in his body was broken.

The Phillies, as an opponent, contributed to Reiser's litany of physical self-punishment. In a Phillies-Dodgers game from back in April, Ike Pearson gave Reiser one of his stretcher exits by braining him with a fastball.

Reiser had already wrenched his back swinging in spring training[4] and been stabbed in the back by a door of corrugated iron while making a catch at Ebbets Field.[5] Clearly, this man's career, and possibly his life, were at every moment in danger.

A few people had thought baseball had finally killed Reiser when Pearson had come inside on his upper lobe.

"It sounded like a shot," Hy Turkin wrote in the *Daily News*, "and couldn't have dropped him any faster if it really were one."[6]

The pitch struck Reiser on the plastic visor of the helmet the Dodgers had started to wear and deflected into his cheekbone.

The doctors credited the helmet with saving Reiser's skull. No one seemed to suggest how much he'd benefit from wearing one more often, even in non-batting scenarios. Nevertheless, Reiser was able to recover from a bone bruise and a blood clot in his face. He was back in the lineup a month later, once more playing the Phillies and once more facing Pearson on May 26.

This wasn't just another Dodgers beatdown of the Phillies until their knuckles were blue. This was now good versus evil. Light versus dark. God's smiling face against a heartless, cackling devil. The New York press was more than happy to cast the roles themselves: Reiser, the "clean-cut young hero from Missouri," and Pearson, the "villain in Philadelphia clothing."

Reiser had already knocked in a run on a sac fly, thanks to an error on Phillies right fielder Johnny Rizzo. The Phillies had bashed their way back into things, though, when Nick Etten tripled in the fourth and Bobby Bragan brought him in with a sac fly.

It was tied up at 4-4 when Reiser came to the plate to face Pearson; the cleanest, cutest Missouri boy you ever did see, like he'd paddled downriver to the game on a raft. The bases were loaded and with two outs, Reiser had a chance to humiliate Pearson by breaking the game wide open. Pearson had a chance, too—a chance to brain Reiser again. But for some reason his urge to kill had subsided. He threw another fastball, this one in a more hittable spot than inside Reiser's skull, and Reiser took a big swing.

He crushed the pitch 400 feet. The ball evaded fielders and clattered off the wall with confounding physics. The Phillies defense showed off its typical baseball instincts as Reiser raced around the bases, and by the time they'd finished their committee meeting and gotten the ball back to the infield, Reiser had slammed home plate with his foot. His inside-the-park grand slam brought blessings upon the land and ended Pearson's reign of terror.[7]

Reiser's hero's journey obviously dominated the headlines of Brooklyn's victory, but the Phillies had also helped the Dodgers along by screwing up two different double play balls in the sixth inning. So, who were the *real* heroes here? The hero who saved the day? Or the ones who heroically *allowed* him to save it?

At this point, the Dodgers beating the Phillies was as inevitable as Doc Prothro cracking open a soda and muttering curses to himself. On May 27, the Dodgers beat them 6-0 the day after Reiser's revenge, and neither team really noticed it had happened.

"Every champion has a sparring partner—a shock absorber who gets hit with everything but the water bucket, falls down, gets up, and goes down again, smiles when he gets socked and never hits the champion more than once in the same spot," Stan Baumgartner wrote. "The Brooklyn Dodgers have the Phillies."[8]

The 6-0 shutout was the Dodgers' eighth straight victory over the Phillies and their fourth straight of the five-game set. Johnny Podgajny got chased early, and every Phillies scoring chance ended with a double play or some stupid thing. The Dodgers put the game out of reach with a broken-bat bloop, a routine grounder to short while the shortstop was covering second, and a line drive that was said to have "gone through" Bobby Bragan.

"Someday the Phillies will beat the Dodgers," Stan Baumgartner theorized. "Maybe it will be in the game tonight."

It wasn't. On May 28, the Phillies gasped and whimpered back from a 5-0 deficit to force a few extra innings out of the Dodgers, but Brooklyn sighed, rolled their eyes, and climbed those dugout steps to victory once again. Pete Reiser hit an RBI double in the twelfth, kicking the defeated Ike Pearson's skeleton as he rounded first base.

In game five, the Phillies had gotten one more chance to prove they were worth more than a chuckle. They were a ball team, damn it; not just some bunch of guys in matching outfits for whom you could face genuine criticism for not beating badly enough. And they'd get their chance to salvage their dignity from beneath a heap of demoralizing losses by taking on a familiar foe once again: Kirby Higbe.

Higbe had the opposite of thrived in Brooklyn, as was typical for the kind of player he was. A "problem child," Stan Baumgartner called him, claiming that Doc Prothro had needed to be a "master handler of problem children" to handle Higbe, whom the Phillies' manager had "coaxed, cajoled, babied, patted on the back and otherwise mothered ... into his many triumphs with the Phils."[9]

Higbe had not found a similar bond with his new skipper, Leo Durocher, who was known more for not taking anyone's bullshit and occasionally having extramarital affairs with famous actresses. This, along with a sore arm with which Higbe had entered the season, was culminating in less effective pitching and more stomping and glove-throwing from Higbe than the Dodgers had hoped.

Higbe would face Tommy Hughes and his head full of regrets on a Wednesday night under the lights at Shibe Park. Hughes, unlike his Dodgers counterpart, was riding high as the Phillies' star rookie flinger. He'd escaped the mines of Pennsylvania coal country with a sharp curve and a blistering heater. Thanks to the patience of Doc Prothro, Hughes would stir excited whispers among the otherwise woebegone Phillies news of the calendar year.

Sure, Hughes had just faced the Dodgers a few days before, and yes, he'd allowed 12 hits and seven earned runs and five walks. But he was young and had showed some promise earlier in the season, and, well. People have to heap their unreasonable expectations onto *somebody*.

It was announced that Hughes would be honored at an event called "Tommy Hughes Day" on June 8 between the games of a doubleheader against the Pirates at Shibe Park. It was not a holiday on the same level as Memorial Day, yet, and would likely not be the biggest draw in town, but it was an honor nonetheless. Students from the Ashley, Pennsylvania schools Hughes had attended near Wilkes-Barre would present him with gifts, and a special train would run from their town to Philadelphia that day for the game. While they were in town making arrangements before the big day, residents of Hughes' hometown took Phillies representatives on a tour of their local coal mine, as if to prove that they were accustomed to lowering themselves.[10]

On May 28, Hughes would get the ball for the 1941 Phillies' first night game of the season, as well as what would become their closest attempt to beating the Dodgers thus far. It didn't look that way when Brooklyn was up 5-0 in the fifth.

Yes, a Phillies error on a grounder to first base allowed a run to score. And *yes*, Hughes was gone by the end of the fifth. But when Higbe came back out for the sixth, the Phillies' Emmett Mueller greeted him with a lead-off homer and Joe Marty slugged a two-run single. The Phillies put together another rally in the ninth to tie the game at 5-5, and in doing so, successfully "prolonged the agony of losing another to the Dodgers."[11]

Durocher pulled Higbe from the game after six innings, and Higbe's reaction was classic: He first performed his favorite move—angrily ripping off his glove—only this time, it wasn't the ground that was his intended target when he threw it, but Durocher himself. There are people in baseball who would say storming off the mound before your manager can give you a pat on the back is bad form. Whipping your glove at him is viewed even less favorably.

"Fortunately for his pocketbook, his control off the mound was as poor as it had been on the mound," wrote Baumgartner, who was really on fire that day. "A strike at that stage would probably have been a costly one."

Prothro had been using his bullpen with fragile success thus far after Hughes' departure. He brought in reliever Roy Bruner to keep the Phillies in the game as it went into extras. Bruner, along with Ike Pearson and Frank Hoerst, were considered Prothro's best weapons coming out of the pen. "Best," is, of course, a relative term, but at this point, it wasn't about the numbers. It was about who could distract the Dodgers long enough for the Phillies to sneak past them.

The Phillies' best chance had come in the bottom of the eleventh with two men on and no outs. Phillies catcher Bennie Warren had bounced a hard grounder off Pee Wee Reese's chin. It looked like the Phillies' face-smashingly good luck was continuing, until the ball trickled into the radius of Dodgers second baseman Billy Herman, who picked it up and turned a double play. Prothro, out of pinch hitters, had to send Bruner out there to hit for himself and watched the reliever hack the last of the Phillies' hopes right back at the pitcher.

Bruner was able to pitch through the tenth and eleventh, but he issued a fatal walk to lead off the twelfth, which meant he'd have to face that young Dodgers stud, Pete Reiser. Reiser doubled off the wall to give his team a 6-5 lead, the ball striking the surface only about half as hard as Reiser would have thrown his own body into it.

The Dodgers' five-game sweep of the Phillies heading into the weekend was just what Brooklyn needed to get back on track. Dodgers first baseman Dolph Camilli hadn't hit a home run since May 10 when he hit another one off Tommy Hughes. The Phillies were able to break through against Kirby Higbe, getting a small, unsatisfying amount of revenge of their own, before they once again lost. Even more impressive was in the eighth inning when Bennie Warren chased a pop-up to the dugout railing, flipped over it, plummeted six feet, and cracked his head. He climbed out of that hole a better ballplayer and one inning later hit the game-tying single off Higbe.

In the Brooklyn write-up, writer Hy Turkin called the Phillies "no pushovers" for the fight they showed in one out of five baseball games, at least leaving behind one very generous compliment as the Dodgers packed up and headed out of town. With them went the one thousand Dodgers fans who had come to Philadelphia wearing six-inch pins that announced with the corniest of glee, *"I'll tell the world I'm from Brooklyn!"*[12]

As the Phillies played the Dodgers five days in a row, losing every game and watching their potentially brain-damaged catcher make a fruitless, last-ditch effort to salvage their dignity before his brain finished filling with blood, Joe DiMaggio had six hits in three games.

Imagine all the people watching DiMaggio play, with no knowledge of what the Phillies were doing. What pure, simple lives they lived, seeing the sport executed with near perfection every day without flubbed grounders and dented skulls. DiMaggio was most prolific on May 28, when his four-hit game saved the Yankees the embarrassment the Phillies seemed incapable of avoiding. Against the Senators, who were struggling to not lose their ninth straight game, DiMaggio homered and singled three times, all of which went to good use. The Yankees built a 9-1 lead in a game they wound up winning 10-8.

The Senators' only hope at salvation came after the loss was already in the books. At one point during the game, somebody threw a ball onto the field.

"Time!" the umpire yelled.

Nobody heard him, or nobody cared, because the Washington pitcher went into his delivery anyway and the Yankee batter smacked a single. Senators skipper Bucky Harris argued that the hit shouldn't have counted because time had been called. Presumably, someone explained to him that the Yankees' private baseball rules exist *outside* of time, and therefore whatever they did on the field *was* the rule.

The runner didn't come in to score anyway. Nevertheless, Harris used the moment to protest the game and its outcome. What this established was that the Yankees *had* won 10-8 and the Senators *had* lost 10-8, but if Harris were to find a sympathetic party to hear his cries, perhaps neither the win nor the loss would exist, which could potentially impact anyone with an ongoing hit streak. No one seemed particularly concerned about this happening, least of all DiMaggio, whose hit streak continued the next day anyway, when he logged his 13th straight game with a knock.[13]

DiMaggio was on his way to becoming part of the fabric of American popular culture, and the country was on its way to falling in love with this man, much like how a teenaged Judy Garland had fallen in love with a 30-year-old composer she was now engaged to marry.

Life continued outside the Phillies. As the city proclaimed itself firmly against the evil on the march in Europe, over 12,000 Philadelphians gathered at the Save Freedom Rally at Convention Hall in support of any and all measures of the United States to defeat the Axis powers overseas.[14]

Things hit a slight hiccup when the piano player decided to play a German drinking hymn as part of their set, but speech-givers asked those in attendance to do for America what they could not for the Phillies: Believe.[15]

May 29

The Dodgers and Giants were preparing to play their first doubleheader of the season after Memorial Day weekend 1941, kicking off the summer with a pair at the Polo Grounds. Over 60,000 fans were expected through the turnstiles, with only the restrictive policies of the fire and police departments standing in their way. The current MLB attendance record—63,000, also set by the Dodgers and Giants—was expected to be old news by the end of the day.

This made Brooklyn, in one columnist's view, the new epicenter of baseball. It's not where the teams would be playing *this* time, and it was vastly outsized by every other stadium in New York, but the Dodgers had just won nine in a row. It was Brooklyn's turn to be America's baseball town, something their fans would be screaming at Giants manager Bill Terry all weekend after Terry had recently said that the Cardinals were the best team in the National League.

"Our reticent Dodger rooters would never point out that if the Phillies were on the visiting end of a Memorial Day doubleheader, Mr. Terry's boys might play before less than half this number," wrote Jimmy Wood in the *Brooklyn Eagle*.[1]

Once again namechecked as the league-wide example of a team no one wants to watch, you'd think at some point it would become bulletin board material for the Phillies—motivation to make their haters eat shit. But the Phils would be catching strays like that for the rest of the decade and in response would shrug and then generally lose again.

Somehow more insulting than the direct insults were the passive ones. The Dodgers had just beaten the Phillies five times in a row, which was covered as though the Dodgers had lost the pennant.

Philadelphia Phillies Vito Tamulis and Stan Benjamin in front of the screen at Braves Field. (Courtesy of the Boston Public Library, Leslie Jones Collection)

"The Dodgers at the moment, own but do not boast of a five-game winning streak," wrote Brooklyn columnist Tommy Holmes. "One thing certain is that they had better play better ball in the immediate future than they did against the Phillies. Dozing fitfully on a meandering milk train in the wee small hours of this morning, the boys had plenty of opportunity to reflect upon their sins of omission and commission in their latest set at Shibe Park."[2]

Again, this was about a five-game winning streak that was part of a bigger eight-game winning streak.

In the days that followed, the scenes were set for another summer: The Yankees would have a game end in a tie due to rain, then pop up to Boston for a doubleheader.

DiMaggio's streak would be subsisted by singles as they moved on to D.C., barely getting in his daily hit against the Senators in a rain-shortened contest and logging only one of the Yankees' two hits in a 13-0 loss.

Kirby Higbe would get his swagger back in the Dodgers' ninth straight victory on June 1, beating the first-place Cardinals.

Plans for Tommy Hughes' special day at Shibe Park progressed.

Roy Bruner would be contacted by his local draft board.[3]

The Phillies were 18.5 games out of first.

Part Two: June

June 1–3

At 16 years old, Joe DiMaggio had been his father's last hope. Well, not really; he had four other sons. But the Sicilian fisherman had already lost one of them, Vince, who had gotten so into baseball and girls that he was not interested in spending time on fishing boats like his father, where there was very little baseball and almost no girls.

But Joe was so terrified of girls that he'd blast through the screen door at full speed if he heard any of his sisters' friends in the house, according to his biographer Richard Ben Cramer. From his grades to his job prospects to the Joe-shaped holes routinely left in the front door, young Joe was going 0-for-3. His father yearned to teach him the ways of a fisherman, until his mother stepped in and said to leave him alone. And somewhere in the pubescent recesses of young Joe's teenage brain, the diamond … called to him …[1]

At 16 games old, Joe DiMaggio's hit streak was similarly awkward and untested. Quiet. Nobody trusted it. Like DiMaggio had been at 16, it was almost ready to stand on its own, but you wouldn't know it, because everyone was mad at it—not for rejecting the life of a fisherman, but because it wasn't longer and more impressive yet.

DiMaggio was "reported to be in the worst slump he ever suffered in his brilliant career," despite climbing to 18 straight games with a hit after the Yankees' doubleheader on June 1.[2] Everyone was waiting for DiMaggio and the Yankees to get better than they'd been, and they would inappropriately compare their team to whatever global atrocity they chose until that happened.

"While the war-torn countries of Europe are waiting to blast their voices, 'the Yankees are coming,' close followers of New York's bombing

Yanks have the same on the tip of their tongues ..." wrote one columnist, seamlessly blending the disappointment of an underperforming baseball team with the horrors of war.

Legends are built by moment after moment of greatness. But early on, they're just a cluster of stuff. Who knows if that stuff will become great? Maybe it's just luck, or the wind. It's probably better to stay focused on a hitter's past failings until he proves he can really hit the ball again.

Whatever was "wrong" with DiMaggio, hitting safely in 18 straight games hadn't fixed it. His reputation as a hitter had really sunk below legend status, but he'd already reached a level of stardom that gave writers and fans permission to criticize him at all times, even when he was outdoing himself. With only five outfield assists in 1940, he'd matched that total within the first 25 games of 1941.[3]

So things were getting better, but still ... it could all be a mirage born from the Manhattan desert. DiMaggio had been in the league since 1936; the people knew him, but to them, he was just that scrub who'd led the league in various offensive categories every year except 1938, when he'd had the *audacity* to let his OPS sink below 1.000. The legend was forming, but far from complete.

Besides, until DiMaggio's star began to shine brighter, there were plenty of other Yankee legends for the people to turn to; players who had streaks of their own, a lot longer than 18 games, and whose playing careers had ended, allowing their accomplishments to be sealed behind rose-colored glass and any shortcomings glossed over or forgotten.

The next day, Lou Gehrig died.

Perhaps you turned on your radio in Philadelphia on June 1, 1941, looking for a thrilling teleplay or an ad for vegetable water that could cure your eye fungus? A jazzy big-band tune to get your toes tapping or any kind of update on the Brits fleeing from Crete and pulling 15,000 Allied troops back into Egypt?

But oh no! The airwaves had been hijacked by the Pontiff himself, Pope Pius XII, begging for peace.

Things in Europe were only getting worse. Through godly crackles and holy static, the Pope said that the world could not be held hostage by war. Before relinquishing the airwaves, his holiness listed his demands to the rest of the planet:

1. A more equal distribution of the world's material goods.
2. Respect for the inherent rights of the workers.
3. The integrity and well-being of the family.[4]

The world told Pope Pius that it would review his suggestions and get back to him. Pope Pius XII died in 1958, presumably still waiting to hear back.

God wasn't feeling as patient as his vessel in The Vatican come June 1941 and took out his frustrations on the general Philadelphia area with a dank, wet afternoon that really brought out the stink of the city. Nothing makes you feel more unloved than nine innings in the rain, unless you have to play 18.

The Phillies may not have beaten the Cubs on either end of their wet doubleheader on June 1, but at least they lost two different ways.

Once the Pope was done pleading with the world for some kind of sanity, the game was on! It was the seventh inning of the first contest when the Phillies' offense finally came to life. They were down 7-0, but for several exciting minutes, it almost seemed as though they had the pride, the skill, and the gumption of a genuine, big city ball team.

In May of 1940, Bobby Bragan had earned his job as the Phillies shortstop the old-fashioned way: by having the guy in front of him play poorly enough to *lose* his job. Even though at the time Bragan was thought of as a skilled defender with a great arm, no speed, and a twig for a bat, he was named the starting Phillies shortstop after Doc Prothro had proclaimed him so, following an error-free tryout. For the Phillies, if you could field grounders for a while without knocking any of your teeth out or facing the wrong direction, then all you were missing was a uniform.

Bragan kept his starting job into 1941, even though he couldn't hit a curveball. The Phillies were all right with vast talent gaps in a player's skillset, too, as long as the player in question did *something* passably. But despite his job security and his high skill as a fielder, Bragan was not the guy the Phillies wanted at the plate with the game on the line.[5]

Down 7-0 in the fifth of game one against the Cubs on June 1, "on the line" wasn't really how the game could be described. "Not over yet," was more accurate. But Bragan went to the plate anyway because that's what the lineup card said to do and hoped the pitcher didn't have a curveball.

Prior to Bragan's at-bat, the Phillies had begun clustering on base. Nick Etten—who you probably *did* want up with the game on the line—had singled off the Cubs' Charley Root. Root had allowed only four hits to that point, and they had been scattered in four different innings, so loading the bases put the Phillies in a peculiar position with which they were totally unfamiliar. The players likely stood on each of the bags, frantically shrugging at each other, looking for guidance. *What happens when there are no bases left?*[6]

Etten was on third now, after Emmett Mueller had worked a walk and Danny Litwhiler had singled as well. And now it was Bragan's turn.

This at-bat had a lot of meaning in it; at least, the most meaning the Phillies would feel all day, and perhaps all month. They'd just finished the *last* month by losing seven of nine, locking in a fun little 7-17 record for May. It would not be their worst single-month record of the 1941 season by *far*, but it still hadn't done wonders for anybody's mood.

Mid-May had brought out Philadelphia's blossoming flora, and the *Inquirer*'s gardening correspondent had written passionately about the resilience of the peony; how it thrived in harsh cold or intense heat, how it weathered the storms of spring, how it clung to the earth with seasonal beauty and formidable strength. But even the city's most unyielding perennial couldn't survive in the dark forever; even the peonies needed a flash of sunlight to give them the hope to go on.[7]

The Phillies fans, a weathered bunch themselves, battered by the soft, relentless cruelty of America's pastime, so too needed an occasional flash of victory to be sustained. They would finally get one as June got underway. Bragan crushed a line drive to left field, making the score 7-4 and giving the fans left at Shibe Park, their garments damp and their hopes wilted, something to celebrate for one warm moment in the sun.

But it was all soon uprooted. The Phillies kept reaching base when Root walked the next batter and a new pitcher walked the following one. With two men on, technically, the tying run was at the plate. But so were, technically, the next three outs. And it turned out that's all Merrill May, Stan Benjamin, and Hal Marnie were: three straight outs, erasing the threat.[8]

The Phillies never mounted another rally and the Cubs tacked on two more runs for good measure, taking the matinee 9-5.

Not even the Pope can save you when you go down in order with two men on. He *might* have been able to work his magic on the next game, however, which the Phillies only lost 1-0, which is the closest you can be to winning in a loss. But if the Pope could have helped the Phillies that day, then he chose not to. Understandably.

Lee Grissom pitched eight innings thrillingly, trading blows with Cubs starter Jake Mooty in a pretty solid impression of a pitchers' duel. But all it took was a pair of back-to-back doubles in the fifth and they slapped an "L" next to Grissom's name in the paper. His teammates threw in a couple of errors just to make the 1-0 deficit stick.[9]

Also, it was still raining.

The mood damp and the weather gross, it seemed like an odd time to start a win streak, but the Phillies found one the next day, June 2.

It wasn't very long. And it was more of a "stumble" than a "streak." And the Cubs had a litany of injuries. And the Cubs' hard-hitting Lou Novikoff was slumping hard enough that he'd just had his nickname downgraded from "The Mad Russian" to "The Sad Russian."

But a win's a win, and two wins are two wins, and nobody was going to comment on the quality of a win in Philadelphia in the summer of 1941.

The Phillies were 0-5 against the Cubs so far that season, and there was no reason, with Johnny Podgajny on the mound, that the Cubs feared a sudden shift in the trend. Perhaps that was their undoing as Podgajny took the ball and Danny Litwhiler picked up his bat.

The 21-year-old starter was not said to be a severe or violent thrower, but occasionally, or even infrequently, his stuff was good enough it didn't matter. That day, Podgajny showed off for the yawning Shibe Park audience over four duels with fearsome Cubs slugger Hank Leiber.

The Phillies had a slim lead all day on June 2, with Litwhiler homering twice, once in the second and again in the sixth, while the rest of the offense did little more than clap. It was a good time for Podgajny to have to face Leiber, then, with a hitter in his lineup who was actually providing run support and Leiber with a batting average below .200 as he recovered from a broken thumb.

Each of the first three times Leiber came up, the Cubs had put enough runners on base to make him a hero. But each time, Podgajny—whom the *Inquirer* didn't hesitate to point out had been playing in lowly Class C Canadian League ball less than a year before—didn't let Leiber get the ball out of the infield.

With the bases full and one out in the seventh, Podgajny induced a force out at home for out number two. And then came Leiber, 0-for-3 on the day, for the fourth and final time. The only thing bigger than his presence was the assumption that the Phillies were about to start losing.

At this point, the Cubs went to their back-up strategy: bullying. From the dugout, they'd taken notice of Podgajny's stance on the mound before his delivery. They started sharing some sneering commentary with him as he pitched. And while some 21-year-olds might have wilted from the antagonism, or at least "slipped" and fired an oopsie straight into their dugout, Podgajny only got more powerful, the chorus of trash talk fading with every out.

Podgajny gripped the Phillies' one-run lead in the palm of his hand. He'd spread six walks far apart enough to avoid the kind of trouble everyone felt was coming. But once again his demons were gathering on the basepaths, and he'd have to pitch his way past them.

Leiber stood in, eager for the end of his hero's journey. He cracked a grounder that bounced to short, where Bobby Bragan gathered it, relayed to second, and killed the threat. Leiber and his sore thumb returned to the dugout. The Cubs returned to the field. And Podgajny returned to the mound twice more on the day, keeping Chicago quiet until the first victory over Chicago had been secured.

The *Philadelphia Inquirer* said Podgajny had pitched "courageously."[10] The *Chicago Tribune* called it "a tragedy."[11] But baseball's schedule did not include a built-in period of mourning and self-pity for any team following a loss to the Phillies, and so the poor Cubs had to come right back out the next day and face Tommy Hughes.

One writer found a way to connect Lou Gehrig to Hughes' success, claiming that the Iron Horse had been famously friendly to rookies in his day—truly a standout quality. It was an era in which rookies were often abused or ignored, with nothing made easy for them in the big leagues because the veterans saw them as younger, healthier, better-looking threats to their employment. Gehrig had never met or interacted with Hughes, the writer said, but Hughes *was* a rookie, so. Gehrig probably would have been nice to him, too, and isn't that wonderful?

There were few members of the Phillies in 1941 who didn't deserve to have their jobs threatened, but Hughes was one of them. On June 3, the kid got the spotlight after a particularly focused performance against the Cubs.

With the flag at Shibe Park at half-mast for Gehrig's death and not the Phillies' playoff chances like people may have assumed, Hughes faced the Cubs lineup and remained utterly unintimidated. His fastball scorched through the strike zone and eluded bats; his curve danced around their mighty strokes with graceful deceit. And at the end of seven innings, Hughes was still out there on the mound—making him physically closer to the bases than any of the Cubs had been all day.

With a perfect game in progress, those in attendance couldn't have given less of a shit what the Phillies' offense was up to, though they were putting together one of their more impressive performances of the season, too. Nick Etten went 2-for-4 with a double and two RBI, Merrill May had four hits and scored twice, and Bobby Bragan had a couple of knocks and pulled off a hidden ball trick. Joe Marty had been caught in the same wave of illness crashing through the Phillies clubhouse that had caused Johnny Rizzo to drop 19 pounds. He bravely kept his sickness to himself until it was everyone's problem and the trainer told him he couldn't play against the Cubs. But so suddenly high functioning was the Phillies offense that even Marty's replacement in center, Stan Benjamin, hit a double and knocked in a run.[12]

Philadelphia Phillie Stan Benjamin kneeling in front of the screen at Braves Field. (Courtesy of the Boston Public Library, Leslie Jones Collection)

The baseball season is long. Every team, even the worst teams ever, can look like they're figuring it out for one night. This isn't to sit here and, once again, point out that the 1941 Phillies were bad. It's to say that even fans watching their team race directly to the basement and board the door shut from the inside can enjoy watching them for one night, assuming they can forget everything that happened before and will happen after.

But the story of June 3 was Tommy Hughes' first seven innings, which put him six outs from throwing the first Phillies no-hitter in 35 years. By the eighth inning, he was starting to grow weary, and Augie Galan of the Cubs waited patiently as Hughes' curve wobbled and his heater missed enough times to draw a free pass and end Hughes' perfect game. Galan took the walk and the no-hitter went next on Lou Novikoff's single.[13]

Hughes would allow another walk, but those were the only three base runners of the day in the Phillies' 7-0 victory; a day in which Tommy Hughes only grazed history, instead of repeatedly bludgeoning it obnoxiously like Joe DiMaggio was doing every day.

Excitement spilled from the box score into the columns. Did the Phillies have a young stud hurler who didn't just chuck it at the backstop when he got tired? Of course, the only way to craft the "young phenom" narrative around the Phillies was to point out that once Hughes was good enough, he wouldn't *be* on the Phillies anymore:

"For years and years, the Phillies have managed to come up with a youngster whom they could sell to pay off the mortgage on the old family homestead. Fellows like Claude Passeau, Chuck Klein, Kirby Higbe … now they have young Hughes," wrote one columnist.[14]

They certainly did, and the Phillies' 7-0 victory secured by Hughes' arm gave them their second win in a row, matching their season-high for consecutive wins. Hughes' high school coach got some credit for having switched Hughes from a first baseman to a pitcher, and even Doc Prothro got a tip of the cap for sticking with Hughes in training camp when everyone else had said to let the kid walk.[15]

Tragically, as good a pitching performance as Hughes had thrown, Lou Gehrig was still dead.

Babe Ruth was said to weep when he got the news about Gehrig's death on June 2. The Yankees still kept a locker for Gehrig with his name on it in the clubhouse.[16] There were plenty of tales told and memories of Gehrig recalled, like how he'd worked as a soda jerk during spring training as a rookie; when he'd gotten hit in the head with a pitch and ignored a doctor's orders to come out of a game before hitting a home run; that if Wally Pipp had just taken a couple aspirin instead of sitting out with a headache on June 1, 1925, the name "Gehrig" may not be as prominent across baseball.[17]

Gehrig's legend was so big, they felt it from baseball royalty like DiMaggio to its last-place corners in Philadelphia as even the lowly Phillies lowered the flag. After all, Gehrig and his streak recontextualized the Phillies' recent two-game win streak: If winning two games in a row was this hard, imagine playing in 2,130 consecutively.

"[Gehrig] was a great player," Gerald Nugent told reporters, having spent exactly several minutes on his statement. "I'm sorry to hear of his death."[18]

Gehrig presents the figure so many ballplayers want to be: the best, the biggest, the eternal. It is a tier reserved for the singularly elite, and DiMaggio was climbing up there to meet him.

"I'm simply at a loss for words," DiMaggio said.[19]

Gehrig's passing provided a reminder that the word "immortal" was always a lie; death finds everyone, even if it has to make up a whole new way to find you. It's why we have such reverence for legends; becoming one is the only way to beat death.

Ted Williams had once sat on the bench as a young player, watching the Yankees take batting practice, absorbing everything around him. Gehrig was sick by this point, looking worn out and taking his time up the dugout steps, even though nobody knew what was wrong with him yet. Gehrig and DiMaggio were both there for batting practice, as were Frank Crosetti, Charlie Keller, Tommy Henrich, and Bill Dickey.

"A *hell* of a lineup," Williams recalled.

And instead of being an awestruck, gape-mouthed young player staring up at the stars, Williams already had them in his crosshairs.

"I said to myself, 'I *know* I can hit as good as these guys.'"[20]

June 6

Johnny Vander Meer was raised by a pair of pious Dutch immigrants, 30 miles from the cheers of Yankee Stadium. Among the festering North Jersey slime pits he caught ripples of city life from the heart of the Big Apple on radio waves that brought the Yankees to New Jersey. Baseball would be his calling, and in his life, he would do two things very well: throw no-hitters and survive peritonitis.

When he was 14, Vander Meer beat the hole in his bowel with two months in the hospital, and when he was 23, he beat the Dodgers and Braves by not allowing them to hit. When he was 26 in 1941, he combined the two efforts, beating the Phillies like they were a hole in his bowel by almost not allowing them to hit.[1]

Vander Meer had thrown both of his no-hitters two years before, and yet it was still all anyone thought about when they saw his name. The no-hitter is treated as a transcendent accomplishment in baseball. It doesn't matter which team is throwing it, but somewhere around the fourth or fifth, people go from keeping an eye on it to tuning in for it. The dynamic shifts from team vs. team to everybody vs. the pitcher. Allegiances are abandoned or intensified; among the people watching, there are only those who want to see history, and those who want to see a man fail.

Anybody can be the enemy of a pitcher trying to be perfect, even the people there to protect him: The defense behind him. The batters in front of him. The beat writers scoffing at claims of a jinx. The intrusive thoughts wriggling into his brain. The weak little grounder or the soaring Texas Leaguer or the foul ball some dipshit ump calls fair. It's not a game any longer. It's one man and one ball trying to find the next zero.

When a no-hitter is done, it's the kind of thing that elevates a pitcher above their peers and makes their name long remembered. And in 1941, every time he played the Phillies, Johnny Vander Meer had a chance to do it again.

To reiterate how easily no-hit the Phillies could be would be redundant at this point, so we'll just say that when the 1941 season came to a close, the Phillies had scored an average of 3.2 runs per game. The first-place Brooklyn Dodgers *allowed* more runs than that on average (3.7) and still finished with 100 wins.

Baseball had gone into mourning after Lou Gehrig's passing and people were starting to become politely impatient about it starting up again. According to writers several days after his death (writers are always so good at knowing what dead people would have wanted), Gehrig would have wanted the baseball season to continue being played, but the universe certainly didn't. It dumped several days of rain on the northeast.

When the sun came out, and Gehrig's ghost found its seat in the bleachers, he was presumably watching the Yankees. But the Phillies had a game, too, and it was against the world champion Reds. It would be the Phillies' fourth attempt of the season at winning three games in a row.

After a slow start, the Reds had found their way back to winning baseball games, so that put some more pressure on Si Johnson's start against them on June 6. Johnson and the Phillies didn't have the chance to win three games in a row every day, but the low stakes were even higher for the Reds: They had to play the Phillies.

In their own way, the Phillies imposed the biggest threat in the league. Not because they had a high chance of embarrassing you on the diamond, but because they had a *nonzero* chance of beating you on the diamond, which would be, of course, an embarrassment. They were the kind of team that, if you lost to them, it meant more than just a loss; it meant deep introspection about what exactly you were doing with your life. Losing to the worst team in baseball didn't mean *you* were now the worst team, but it did mean that you lost a game you had every reason to win and no excuse to lose.

"… [The Reds'] hopes of success of any kind this season ride on the outcome," penned one writer. "It's almost axiomatic in baseball that 'if you can't beat the Phillies, you can't beat anyone.'"[2]

The Reds were having one of those seasons played under the crushing weight of high expectations. They *had* won the World Series in 1940, after all, and hey, did you hear about these two no-hitters Johnny Vander Meer threw in 1939? Sure, the Reds had stumbled through the spring, but why *not* assume they'd turn it around any day now? They weren't the *Phillies*, for god's sake.

Now, against the most beatable team in probably any sport, Cincinnati was being given another opportunity to turn things around. Should they lose to the Phillies—the goddamn *Phillies*—what else would there be to do but throw their hands in the air and go be coaches at their old high schools?

As the rain cleared and the clouds scattered, each team now faced its equally, incredibly low stakes: in one dugout, the glorious mediocrity of three consecutive wins, and in the other, the threat of self-imposed baseball exile. And it would all be determined by nine innings under the arc lights.

Baseball in the nighttime was still a novel enough concept in 1941 to the point that it was mentioned at least in passing each time it occurred. Sure, electricity and baseball had existed *alongside* each other for years, but now they had been combined into one luminous primetime event. The darkness that had confused and terrified early humans had been once more conquered by our most powerful minds. Now, we did more than stumble about in the dark or hide from it in our shelters—darkness was so unintimidating, we played our novelty games and ate hot dogs while surrounded by it.

In the second inning, with the Phillies down 1-0 on a bomb to deep left served up by Si Johnson, Danny Litwhiler slapped a sharp grounder to short between the defense. Reds shortstop Eddie Joost reached it just before it could touch the outfield grass, but his loose, chaotic grip proved fatal for the play and the ball shot out of his hand, trickling two feet away. By the time he'd recovered it, Litwhiler had beaten out an infield single.

Satisfied with Litwhiler's effort, the Phillies' offense took the rest of the night off.

This Johnny Vander Meer start was not a no-hitter for very long, as Litwhiler's hit had come in the second. But when the game was over, a quick scan of the box score revealed Vander Meer had missed a third no-hitter by only one bad grip on the ball. This revelation retroactively made the Phillies his enemy, as they had prevented the young lefty from doing something objectively great. The Phillies weren't the home team anymore; they were the enemy of greatness. Their hometown paper claimed they'd "ruined" the no-hitter, which would have dominated the news on a day off for Joe DiMaggio.[3]

It was as though the universe, unable to wash the Phillies away, chose instead to counter whatever crumbs of glory had landed in their laps with an equal and exact amount of shame, subtracting what little joy they could from a season everyone already wanted to forget by early June.

It was the Reds' first win against the Phillies in their last five tries, and the Phillies' fourth failed attempt to win three in a row. They wouldn't have the chance to do so again until August 1. They wouldn't successfully do so until August 12.

It would be 14 years until Johnny Vander Meer's next no-hitter.[4]

June 7–9

Hitler was about to get a message from Philadelphia.

No, it was not, "Go Birds." It was the 6,000-ton minelayer called the *Terror*, a sleek vessel built to blow a hole in little Adolf's naval campaign. Launching from the Navy Yard into the Delaware, the stars and stripes flapping in the breeze, the warship was cheered on by patriotic throngs who'd baptized it in champagne.

No one's been anything other than nervous when somebody from Philadelphia shows up. And yet, it was written, the *Terror* "looked anything but her name" as it hit the water, "tip-toe[ing] gracefully as a gazelle."

But there was a "grimness" to the whole event that lingered in the air above the assembled Navy officers, sailors, and "grimy workmen" who'd gathered to see the *Terror* off. The ship had no portholes and a degaussing cable wrapped around its body to ward off enemy mines, reminders of a war's thoughtless, faceless violence. And as a naval officer delivering a speech brutally reminded everyone, "Germany's production of war tools is huge, and there is no one left in the world but the American workman who can out-produce them."[1]

There were constant reminders of the state of the world as it sank into war, and the darkness gathering seemed to put the city in a bad mood. As the summer began, Philadelphia's pulse quickened and slowed through moments of quiet and spasms of violence. In any big city, the population is vast and diverse, migrating through intersections and filling train cars. Never could so many people wake up on the same side of the bed, but they do all get the same weather, the same decisions of the civic leaders lording over them, the same score from the Phillies game yesterday. In one way or another, the mood is shared.

A couple of teenagers vaulted over the counter and attacked the owners of a burger shop at 26th and Brown, violent and hormonal about the size of the hamburgers they'd been served. The garbage piled up in the city's Oak Lane neighborhood on the northern end, and its disgusted residents complained that collection had been spotty since last Christmas. And an attempted launch of the *South Dakota*, a Navy battleship, from the docks in Camden was delayed for 35 minutes to wait for a more agreeable tide and ended with the vessel refusing to move until they threw the hydraulic pumps into overdrive.[2]

Philadelphia was taking some L's. That meant the Phillies had four games against the Pirates to save the city.

Sorry, city.

Pittsburgh was sitting on top of the Phillies at the bottom of the standings. As the Pirates attempted to play their way out of comparisons with the worst team in the league, the Phillies would have four chances in three days to swipe at their ankles from under the cellar door.

On June 7, the Phillies managed to squeeze a single run out of a bases-loaded, one-out situation in the second. Danny Litwhiler had reached base by slapping a grounder at Pittsburgh shortstop Arky Vaughn, who'd gotten a sudden case of the bumbles. Litwhiler eventually came in to score on a sac fly and delivered the Phillies a 1-0 lead, which was all they'd need to win game one. But they added the unthinkable—an *additional* run—and somehow avoided accusations that they were running up the score.

Phillies fans were always learning who their starters were, given Gerald Nugent's common tactic of signing anyone who sent him a letter asking to play for little pay. Therefore, they didn't always know how to read a guy's success on the field. Was he actually good? Was he just streaky? Was today just a good day? *Should* the Phillies trade him before he turns back into a .130 hitter?

Dan Litwhiler had piqued some interest as one of the team's premiere power hitters, then disappeared for a few dozen at-bats, quieting his support section. In the first 32 games of the season, Litwhiler had hit .226, making spectators wonder what happened to that young man who hit safely in 21 straight games the previous September. But in early June, he came crashing through a slump with a pair of bombs against the Cubs, got his average back up to .250, and was ready to start making promises again.

"When the season was just getting underway, Danny predicted he'd hit more than .300," wrote one reporter. "He says he still feels the same way."[3]

Litwhiler suppressed a Pirate uprising in the seventh when a grounder found its way to him in left. He dangerously scooped it up as Pittsburgh's Elbie Fletcher rounded third and Litwhiler fired a shot home. Fletcher was a dead duck with six feet between him and the plate.[4]

"Dangerous" Dan, one writer had called him earlier that year. But don't worry—it wasn't for any scary or cool reasons.

"Don't get the wrong impression, he's not a gun-totin', bank-bustin' desperado," the public was relieved to learn. "He's the latest rookie sensation of the Philadelphia Phillies."

This explanation did little in the way of explaining the "Dangerous" label, but Litwhiler *was* in Philadelphia, where danger could be lurking on the other side of the hamburger counter. The likely answer, however, is that people had decided that "dangerous" was a funny way to describe the wholesome Litwhiler. Besides, a nickname doesn't need to make sense if it is alliterative. Everyone knows this. Joe DiMaggio was never actually electrocuted on the field, but they still called him "Joltin' Joe," and no one ever questioned it.

Sarcastic nicknames aside, the true motivator for the Phillies' 2-0 victory in game one was the purest of baseball stories: revenge.

The Pirates had cut Cy Blanton in 1939. His velocity was too low, his delivery too slow, and his arm was too busted to be of any use. More like "Sigh" Blanton: A habitual screwballer, he began to warn other hurlers away from throwing the pitch, blaming it for his ruination.

"The muscles of his elbow were so badly snarled that he could barely throw a ball and then only with great anguish," read one report.[5]

What kind of team cuts a pitcher just because he can't throw the ball without screaming? The 1939 Pirates, that's who. Fortunately, skilled baseball analyst and guy who definitely didn't just hear that Blanton was released while rummaging through the Pirates' trash Gerald Nugent collected the young man from a Syracuse club and got him in a Phillies jersey prior to the 1941 season.

Blanton (we can only assume while weeping) accepted his fate and put on his new Phillies uniform. But between the locker room and the mound, something changed. The 32-year-old with the elbow cursed by God would not go to his grave having wasted his life in Philadelphia. He would pitch his way out of this hell, one start at a time.

And on June 9, he got to do so against the team that let him go.

On his way to one of two career all-star appearances, the 2-0 win was Blanton's second victory of the 1941 season over the Bucs and improved his record to 5-1, at a time when pitchers' win-loss records were printed without any eye-rolling. His return to form was notable by those in Pittsburgh, too, where it was written that Blanton was an "inspiration for all who have lost hope through adversity."

"Brother, when you deliver like that for the cellar champions, you're a pitcher," read one head-shaking Pittsburgh writer.[6]

The next day, the Phillies lauded their starter with a celebration of another one: Tommy Hughes Day had finally arrived. Announced over a week before, it was time to honor the kid from a town near Wilkes-Barre.

The children from Hughes' hometown had been brought down earlier that day by train and presented him with gifts on the field. The Hanover Township Band, of which Hughes had been a member as a boy, played several numbers to honor him. He got a religious medal, an order for a hat and suit, and a brand-new video camera, all while standing at home plate with his parents.[7]

But on Hughes' mind was probably not all the fun home movies he'd be shooting with his new camera or how much more easily he'd get into heaven with a religious medal around his neck. Rather, he was likely stuck on how moments before, with his parents and 1,200 kids from his hometown watching, he'd given up four earned runs in the ninth in a game the Phillies had lost, 12-2.[8]

For eight frames, Hughes had proven himself worthy of his loved ones taking a two-hour train ride down from Wilkes-Barre. The Phillies' offense even gave him a 1-0 lead off a Joe Marty homer. That put a lot of pressure on Hughes to be perfect on his special day, and for a while, he was.

Then the eighth came together like a surreal nightmare as Hughes watched the bases fill with Pirates. There was the throwing error by Merrill May that let the lead-off man on. There was the walk Hughes issued to the next batter to put a man in scoring position. There was the bunt in front of the plate that Hughes, in a desperate bid for control, tried to snare and fire to third to at least kill the lead runner.

But no. He was too late, the runner was too fast, and Hughes returned to the mound, his parents, friends, and loved ones all wondering when the train back to Wilkes-Barre was leaving.

A bases-clearing double was Hughes' end. The looping RBI single over short that followed it was just obnoxious. Two consecutive walks forced in another run. Looking for any way to stop the bleeding, Merrill May fielded the ball and tried to nail a guy at home. He hit the runner in the back with his throw.

This unfortunate cycle continued for some time. Pittsburgh was a steadily chugging offense machine, and the Phillies had already asked three different pitchers to do something, anything: Hughes was out, Ike Pearson was in; then Pearson was out and Roy Bruner was in. Instead, the Pirates put together a nine-run rally in the ninth. What had been a 3-2 nailbiter going into the final inning was an unwatchable laugher by the time the Phillies came up to bat, too shell shocked to make solid contact.[9]

Then they made Hughes go back out there and stand on the field for a while with his parents.

There was a bit of good news when Johnny Rizzo had a hit in game one. It was not notable on its own, but given the context, it was a sign of man's triumph over disease. Rizzo had missed the last few weeks with "a series of illnesses" that had cut his weight by almost 20 pounds, depending on which report you believed.

"Johnny Rizzo, with a strep infection of the throat, is most seriously sick," came one report a few days prior on the Phillies' status as the most diseased team in the league—Joe Marty also had chills and a fever, Stan Benjamin was weak from a lengthy illness but still playing, and Doc Prothro had been diagnosed with an acute case of not "feeling too chipper."[10]

Having lost a full toddler's worth of body weight, Rizzo's return had not been rushed, but it was welcome, as he logged a hit for this starved offense in the nightcap as well. As Rizzo stood on second after a double, memories flickered feverishly through his head as he recalled something about getting on base with people in Pirates uniforms around. Two years before in 1939, he'd set the single-game Pirates franchise record for RBI with nine against the Cardinals. That season, he would only knock in 55 runs total and hit just six homers—a third of which had come in that game.

Following his nine-RBI outburst, Rizzo had settled into a nice, quiet, mediocre career with the Phillies; one destined to end a year later with Brooklyn in 1942. But at least he'd leave baseball with a bat in his hands and not shivering on a hospital bed, talking to dead relatives.[11]

Like the Reds, Giants, and any other team with a scrap of dignity, the Pirates came to Philadelphia expecting to win. Four games at Shibe Park meant four chances to climb up the standings. And with half the Phillies coughing and flop sweating and the other half not feeling too chipper about it, anything less would be a disappointment. But Pittsburgh *did* leave the Shibe Park disappointed, their 12-2 thumping of Hughes in front of his loved ones nullified by the victory the Phillies were able to pull off in game two.

Johnny Podgajny was the game two starter. He was his typical careful self around the strike zone, not wanting opposing hitters to be too overwhelmed by his fastball over the plate. But the difference was that this time, his plan actually worked. Part of that was his performance, and part of it was the defense behind him.

Danny Litwhiler was feeling dangerous that day. But what didn't feel dangerous when a man named DiMaggio stepped to the plate in 1941? Fortunately, in this case it was just Vince, Joe DiMaggio's brother who played for the Pirates, in the middle of his most recent 0-for-4 day. At one point he took a swing and tagged one to left that started drifting … drifting … drifting into foul territory.

Litwhiler followed it from the outfield all the way to the foul line, and with a lower back-devastating lean, lurched his arm forward to make a spearing catch of DiMaggio's wandering pop-up. The Shibe Park crowd awoke, wiped the peanut shells off their laps, and rose in celebration of a well-executed play by someone wearing a Phillies uniform.

But Litwhiler wasn't done. The game entered heartbreak territory in the eighth, with the Phillies' small lead constantly under threat. Sure, they hadn't let the Pirates chip away all afternoon, but there was still the possibility of losing very quickly, or all at once.

The Phillies had suspiciously built a 5-1 lead, but Pittsburgh scored in the sixth to make it a 5-2 game. With a runner on second, the Pirates were again menacing Phillies pitching with a relentless attack. So relentless, it felt, that the Pirates' own base runner assumed that a hard-smacked fly ball was a sure-thing double over Danny Litwhiler's head.

Litwhiler, presumably pulling down a pair of cool shades and whispering, "It's time to get *Dangerous*" to himself, chased the ball to the fence in left field, caught it, turned, and gunned down the Pirates runner trying to get back to second. Once again, the Shibe Park faithful had to give it to him: On two different chances to humiliate himself, Litwhiler had done the opposite and made Phillies fans proud. It was something the city rarely saw and the fans likely calloused their hands with applause, so unfamiliar a feeling it was to bring palm to palm in celebration.

On four hits, Podgajny's start, and Litwhiler's live wire arm, the Phillies took game two, 5-2, and left Shibe Park with the day not totally ruined, unless you asked Tommy Hughes how things had gone.

"One Win, Anyway," read the *Inquirer*'s unimpressed headline.[12]

The Phillies had found it within themselves to steal two out of three games from the Pirates on the homestand, with one more game remaining. The finale would be their chance to truly embarrass the city of Pittsburgh, and the Pirates would have their last opportunity to look at themselves in the mirror without crying. Once more, beating or not beating the Phillies would determine an opposing team's self-worth, and the Pirates put all their hopes and dreams for the near future in the hands of a rookie named Aldon Wilkie making his second career start.

Of course, anyone who's spent significant time watching the Phillies in *any* generation knows that nothing can shut down their offense like an inexperienced, unimpressive pitcher the team has never seen before. And those people would not be surprised in regards to what happened next.

Wilkie took the bats out of the Phillies' hands, except for one moment in the fifth when the Phillies accidentally loaded the bases with no outs but—you guessed it—couldn't work out the math to score. Lee Grissom took a hissing liner off the wrist and yet another Phillies' name was scribbled on a chart at Temple Hospital.[13] The Phillies lost, 5-0.

Tommy Hughes' parents had gone home, thankfully, but there was another guest of honor at Shibe Park: Connie Mack had left his Athletics on the road and returned to Philadelphia to pick up an honorary degree from the Pennsylvania Military College earlier that morning. As one does.

Mack seemed to understand why his Athletics had looked so imperfect in 1941 as well: It was partially, he explained, because Cleveland had come out of spring training much hotter than anyone had expected them to be and proven much more formidable for the A's to handle in their frequent meetings. And because it was Connie Mack who said it, no one rolled their eyes and called it an excuse. If the Phillies had explained all their losses in 1941 by claiming that they were the other team's fault for being better than them, it would have been viewed less as an insight and more as an objective reality.

But despite the loss, the Phillies could pack up and hit the road with a series split; a momentum builder for their squad and a mark of immeasurable shame on the Pirates. Sure, they'd been shut out by a Canadian in the last game, but a team like the Phillies needed a short memory to get through the long, long season. Once you started comparing them to other, better teams, their isolated accomplishments never looked as good.

For example, in New York, the Yankees continued playing their boring brand of predictable baseball: They scored five runs in the ninth, thanks in part to a hard-hit RBI from DiMaggio, and came from behind to win. They swept a doubleheader against the Browns with DiMaggio hitting three of their seven home runs on the day. The Yankees had an off day, so to fill the media's daily DiMaggio quota, a story was run nationally about the best swings in baseball, with DiMaggio nearing the top of the list.

The story contained zero Philadelphia Phillies.[14]

Yawn.

June 10–11

Ladies Day at Shibe Park! A special game set aside by the Phillies and Athletics to acknowledge that even women, with their eyeballs and capacity for happiness, could witness and enjoy baseball, a game they would not be allowed to play professionally until a war took all the men.

Over the years, the promotion created plenty of memorable moments across the sport. In 1947, the Yankees came to Shibe Park to play the A's on Ladies Day. Their starter, Bobo Newsom, tipped his cap to the crowd as he was booed, threw balls into the stands, and successfully baited the Athletics' third base coach into a fist fight, twice.[1]

A man jumped up in the Shibe Park stands on Ladies Day in 1938, grabbing frantically at his own ass, having accidentally set off a book of matches in his pants. In what had to have been the real-life version of a nightmare he'd had once, the man then had to take his pants off in front of everyone on Ladies Day to avoid severe burns on his crotch and butt.[2]

And *The Chester Times* out of Delaware was tickled pink by a question it received from a female fan in 1946: "Is there a woman's baseball game in Philadelphia today?" she asked.

"Do you mean, 'Is it Ladies Day at Shibe Park?'" they giddily corrected her.

She had of course meant "Is it Ladies Day at Shibe Park," but the newspaper wrote up a tittering recap of the exchange, their condescension a Ladies Day tradition as well.

Ladies Day started bright and early for the 1941 Phillies on June 10. Something about scoring fewer than 10 runs combined in their last six games had Doc Prothro feeling less than confident. He informed his offense they would be arriving at 10 a.m. before their game against the Cardinals to collect their thoughts.

The Phillies got up with the earthworms and for two hours Prothro had them trying to remember how to hit a baseball. The earthworms probably had a more productive morning, and the Phillies scored as many times in action against the Cardinals as they had during batting practice.[3]

Heinie Mueller led off the game with a liner to right. Later in the ninth he hit another liner, miraculously tracked down by the Cardinals' Don Padgett. In between those two hits, the Phillies had no hits. And one of those hits wasn't a hit.

It was Cardinals starter Lon Warneke who'd flummoxed the Phillies lineup this time, a child of the Ouachita Mountains who'd grown into one of the most dominant curveballers in baseball. He got his first gig in pro ball when his hairdresser sister passed his name along to one of her clients, the wife of a Texas League team owner. In 1941 he'd throw four shutouts and no-hit the World Series-champion Reds in Cincinnati.

The following year, 1942, he would begin to show signs of decline, and when Warneke admitted he felt the end was near, he was traded from the Cubs to the Cardinals. He then faced the minimum number of batters in a two-hit performance, once more against the Reds. It was considered the greatest pitching performance of 1942.[4]

Warneke was too good to have done anything other than play baseball. As a young player, a scout for Cleveland had seen him pretending to row a boat on the field during a rainstorm and deemed him too silly of a goose for a big-league deal. At the end of the season, Warneke was named co-MVP of his team and signed a deal with Chicago.

One coach watched Warneke play and told him he'd never make it as a first baseman. On a hunch, he had Warneke pitch. He was so good they signed him to a deal. Later, Warneke was getting smacked around in the minors until a teammate noticed that he was looking at the ground instead of the catcher's mitt at the end of his delivery, skewing his accuracy. Warneke corrected himself and was soon unhittable.[5]

Somehow, no matter what path he'd have taken, Warneke's fate clashed with that of Phillies hitter Heinie Mueller. The year before his match-up with Warneke, in a game against the Cardinals, Mueller had started jogging off the field during a live play, not realizing he'd been called safe. This cascaded into a bumbling display of basepath buffoonery that ended with both Mueller and another Phillies base runner being called out.

Mueller's baserunning boobheadedness had melted another lobe off Doc Prothro's brain causing the skipper to mutter, "I just turned 47, but after plays like this I may not make it to 48."[6] That sentiment would be more famously paraphrased by Eddie Sawyer after he quit following the 1960 Phillies losing their first game, "I'm 49 years old and I want to live to be 50." Something about managing the Phillies really makes people think about the immediacy of their mortality.

With his death a day closer on June 10, 1941, Prothro watched Mueller crack a first-inning single and looked forward to a productive day of offense. He was promptly bunted over to second base, for an early chance in scoring position. He'd be the last Phillies runner to get that far all day.

Warneke took the lead-off hit personally. After working around Mueller in the first, he induced lazy flies and meaningless pop-ups, not even granting the Phillies the dignity of a hard-hit ground ball. Warneke no-hit the Phillies for the rest of the day as Prothro waited impatiently for the cold hand of death on his shoulder.

As Warneke threw everything but his shoe at the Phillies, Si Johnson had been tasked with opposing him. Warneke sent Johnson a message, too, by singling a pitch right back at him in the third inning. The hit started a rally that got St. Louis two of its three runs, and Warneke got to show off his speed, too, scoring from second on a double. It's easy to imagine him doing all of this without breaking an intense stare at Johnson or Mueller, whoever he felt was a bigger obstacle to his personal success at the moment.

"Could it be that so many one-hitters are pitched at Shibe Park because the Phillies are the opposition?" asked one columnist, slowly catching up with everybody else.

The Phillies weren't one-hit the next day on June 11, and instead unloaded a relatively strong, offensive response to the previous day's misfire. But it was not strong or even close to offensive enough to take a lead over the Cardinals—an uncharacteristically pulse-pounding pitchers duel was still locked at 2-2 in the tenth inning.

The Phillies had tried everything to win: putting runners on base but not knocking them in, successfully knocking them in but an umpire blowing the call, Heinie Mueller hitting the ball hard but exclusively for outs. None of these terrible plans worked and they lost, 3-2.[7]

The Phillies' best had still managed to come up short. There was a lot of that going around baseball. Fortunately for the rest of baseball, nobody was giving and getting less than the Phillies.

Though something was definitely off in Chicago: Midway through the Yankees' game against the White Sox, Joe DiMaggio was 0-for-3. He grounded out with a man on in the first. He killed a Yankees rally with the bases loaded in the third. And he grounded out in the middle of a scoring threat in the sixth, being relegated to moral support when his teammate, Frankie Crosetti, played the hero of the day with a grand slam.

DiMaggio came up in the seventh with the Yankees still sporting a 5-0 lead. The tension when a crowd was still waiting for DiMaggio's hit of the day was becoming concern that they would be the audience for the streak's demise. He'd probably get another at-bat at this point, the way the Yankees had been hitting the White Sox, but he was running out of chances to … do the thing nobody wanted to say out loud.

The public was becoming aware of the situation with DiMaggio. His hit streak, now at 24 games, had reached the point at which it warranted mention at the end of recaps when a reporter would dump out the rest of their notebook. Of course, the Yankees themselves were barely a presence in the American League, a mere seven games over .500 at 29-22 and seemingly stuck in *second place* behind Cleveland. Can you imagine? A team so bad it couldn't even be in first place for the entire season?

Conversations about the All-Star Game had already started and there was concerned talk about the Yankees not filling every position on the American League roster.

"It's certainly going to be strange to see so few Yankees on the squad," lamented one columnist who'd likely been shuddering as he wrote. "But maybe four weeks will change the picture."[8]

Yes, thankfully there was still time for New York to quit this embarrassing charade as a *second*-place team and for certain superstars to elevate their hitting streaks to more historic levels.

DiMaggio shoved a ground ball to deep third base that spread the defense far enough apart for Joe to jolt his way to first. The Yankees were spared the embarrassment of a player failing to maintain a historic offensive pace, and DiMaggio's *next* chance to blow his streak wouldn't be until tomorrow.

In his last at-bat of the day, he grounded into a double play.

The world around him was changing. DiMaggio's teammate Tommy Henrich was starting to carry the offense as DiMaggio struggled to get a ball out of the infield. Henrich's batting average had jumped 60 points in the last 30 days and he'd matched DiMaggio, dinger for dinger, each of them hitting four in the Yankees' last nine games. Henrich's home run total for the season so far, nine, matched his total from the entirety of 1940, with most of the summer still to come. All because he'd made one little change.

When Henrich had started the season in a lousy slump, he'd started toying with lighter and heavier bats. One day, trying another new stick, he managed to bop a pair of singles into the outfield, despite not hitting them squarely.

"But they were base hits," Henrich said. "I was willing to settle for anything."[9]

He looked down at the cumbersome stick in his hands. It was one of DiMaggio's.

DiMaggio was five hits away from the Yankees' all-time consecutive game hit streak. It turned out all Henrich had needed to fix his swing was the bat DiMaggio was using to break an all-time hitting record.

It contained immense power and some kind of devilry. Even the things that had nothing to do with the bat, like DiMaggio's newfound ability to draw more walks, were credited to the bat. Obviously, some of DiMaggio's natural essence had made its way from his hands into the bat and then spread into Henrich, giving him sounder judgment and a quicker swing. Now DiMaggio's hitting was so potent that it was making *other* players better.

But Yankees fans are famously fickle. As DiMaggio's hit streak reached the quarter-century mark, it had to be asked, was the streak starting to lose its sexiness? After all, it was just one guy trying to do the same thing every night. And he hadn't even been doing it *that* successfully.

Somebody at the *Daily News* started to wonder what pitchers were giving up all these hits to DiMaggio—in the American League, the Yankees didn't have the luxury of playing the Phillies every couple of weeks, but they did get to knock down pushovers like the Washington Senators and St. Louis Browns pretty frequently.

The numbers were crunched. DiMaggio was hitting .577 against the Athletics, .455 against the Browns, and .351 against the Senators. The rest of the AL's pitching staffs didn't see him as much more than a regular threat—the Tigers really had him tamed, as DiMaggio had gone just 6-for-29 against them in six games.[10]

The publishing of this information seemed to be an attempt to reestablish that DiMaggio was just a human. Sure, he was performing an impressive and ongoing feat, but … maybe it was all in his bat? Maybe he was just a normal hitter having a good couple of weeks? Maybe now it was Henrich's turn to be the nation's Yankee darling while DiMaggio was hitting stupid ground balls to third?

Rumor was Joe's older brother, Vince, could be headed to Brooklyn from Pittsburgh in a Pirates-Dodgers trade. Soon, there could be *two* DiMaggios in New York. Maybe that could reinvigorate their brand. Or maybe Joe could keep hitting safely through the summer solstice. That would also probably work.

But if writers wanted to talk about baseball being played disappointingly, they didn't need to tear down one of the game's stars. While there's nothing better for media engagement than a ferocious pile-on of a beloved figure, the Phillies would always be there to receive ridicule whenever the writers had a few spare insults left over.

Whether it was DiMaggio or the Phillies, they needed to get their licks in *now.* Teams got better all the time. They make the right trade, play the right back-up, and suddenly their fortunes would improve. There was no reason, other than their entire recent history, to think the Phillies weren't capable of a turnaround by giving their roster a boost.

While the Yankees talked about upgrading their roster in a potential deal for Washington's Sid Hudson or Dutch Leonard, the Phillies let it be known that they were also not afraid to make a move. Anymore.

"PHILS ACQUIRE GIANT," read the very small headline reporting the news, and for once, they were describing a large person and not the ballclub from New York.[11]

Bill Harman had been a Cavalier at the University of Virginia—*the* Cavalier, it seemed, as he'd served as president of the student body and graduated with both honors and a Bachelor of Science. He was six-foot-four, weighed 200 pounds, and upon signing his Phillies contract, he instantly became the tallest catcher in the major leagues. He could also pitch.[12]

But that wasn't all. The Phillies—*Gerald Nugent's* Phillies—had actually *outbid* several teams to get Harman, including Cleveland, Detroit, and ironically, the Giants. Truly, a new day had dawned in Philadelphia; one in which the Phillies would spend money on a player intended to improve the ball club, pushing past several other teams to do so.

That new day dawned for Philadelphia the way days were always dawning for the Yankees, and it all started with a giant one-man pitching battery.

Harman's major-league career would last five games. He'd wow onlookers by pitching in the first game of a doubleheader and catching in the second.[13] He'd help the Phillies four-hit the U.S. Army 44th Division's baseball team in July in an exhibition to embarrass our men in uniform.[14] Once again, promise had began to grow out of a decision these new Phillies had made, one that validated their signing and made a better future possible for both the team and its newest star.

Then Harman allowed eight runs in 13 innings as a pitcher, went 1-for-14 at the plate as a hitter, and the Phillies lost every game in which he played. His last game in the majors was September 23.

Ah, well.

Maybe a new day will dawn again tomorrow.

June 14–16

The drama was too much. At least when Babe Ruth had been setting the single-season home run record, he hadn't needed to hit one every game. One bad day at the plate and DiMaggio's run would come to a devastating end, and the news would go back to being all about the sweaty little fascist marching across Europe and when this DiMaggio bum was going to finally get his head out of his ass and be one of the greatest players of all time.

Doc Prothro, despite his dedication to dentistry, was a soda fiend. Kirby Higbe clocked Prothro at drinking 20 Cokes a day. He was probably on number 15 or 16 of the afternoon when he'd exclaimed earlier in the spring that he had the best young pitching staff in the majors.

The writers who had caught an early glimpse of the Phillies' young pitcher Johnny Podgajny had rave reviews: He was a quick worker who didn't let hitters get comfortable, thanks to a sweeping curve and a fastball Stan Baumgartner called "corking."

But by mid-June, things hadn't changed. The Phillies were 17-36. They were in last place. Doc's pitching staff was either not the staff he'd said they were or he had just been totally wrong about them. In any case, Podgajny wasn't feeling like a hotshot.

Pitching against the Cubs on June 15, he gave up a triple and two singles to start the fifth. A run had come across to make it 6-0. Podgajny got the ball back and was visibly frazzled enough for everyone to know how he was feeling.

Phillies third baseman Merrill May left his post and jogged over to Podgajny on the mound, telling the kid one thing:

"Don't give up."

Something twitched on Podgajny's face.

The Phillies heard "don't" a lot in 1941, often from writers and fans: *They don't hit. They don't field. They don't pitch. They don't even open all the concession stands or seats at their home games.*

"Speaking of the DiMaggio streak, the Phillies don't get excited until somebody goes 46 games *without* a hit," wrote a quip master at the *Louisville Times.*[1]

Perhaps it was because Podgajny was new to the scene that he became so perturbed at the word "don't." For anybody who'd been playing, or even just watching the Phillies for the past few years, this was about the time when they would settle into their groggy summer dirt nap, accidentally winning a game every 10 or 12 days or so.

They had just lost five in a row and been shut out in four of them. They had scored two runs total in their last five games. Podgajny was pitching in game two of a doubleheader, so they had already been shut out once that day, a game in which Tommy Hughes had given up a bunch of runs in the first. The Phillies were shut out for nine innings by Claude Passeau, another former pitcher of theirs who'd moved onto better things, including three straight all-star seasons, starting in 1941.

On June 14, the day before Podgajny's appearance, the role of "beleaguered Phillies starter" had been played by Cy Blanton, the man who had battled back from having his arm muscles shredded before being cut by the Pirates, was still on the Phillies' pitching staff, waiting to be kicked off the bus or executed in a field or however a team within striking distance of last place gets rid of its unwanted players.

The Cubs had only successfully completed three shutouts by mid-June 1941, and surprisingly, only one had been against the Phillies, back at the beginning of the month. They'd get numbers four and five in one day not because of any shortcomings by Blanton, who allowed only five hits and a pair of runs before a rainstorm swept the players off the field. In fact, Chicago barely had to even score to get their third run—Frank Hoerst and Ike Pearson combined to load the bases with walks, and the Cubs needed only a routine ground-out to bring in an insurance run.

Blanton, like many pitchers before him, had been let down by the Phillies' offense, which had done very close to nothing against the Cubs'

Vern Olsen, a pitcher they'd faced less than two weeks prior and scored six runs in the first three innings off him. Merrill May had four hits that day.

But May wasn't doing any pitcher any favors on June 14 and went hitless, with Olsen allowing only three hits between two Phillies, Emmett Mueller and Bobby Bragan. It was his second straight shutout.

After Podgajny's implosion the next day, morale was starting to bottom out. A story in the *Cincinnati Enquirer* had the Phillies requesting a $100,000 loan to stay afloat. How could this happen? The same way it always had. Other teams, reminded of the Phillies' existence, seemed to always go back to the same point, as it kept being valid: The Phillies don't have good enough players, and when they do, they find a way to lose or sell them.

Their two best from 1940, Kirby Higbe and Hugh Mulcahy, had shipped out in a swap with Brooklyn and a one-way deal with the U.S. Army, respectively. Prothro had plenty of defenders in the press, claiming he was an excellent manager; he just always had teams that were more than an excellent manager away from success. And it seemed like Prothro had already started experiencing symptoms beyond low morale.

Prothro told the press a story from 1940, in which his Phillies had been simply *outdoing* themselves in one particular game, getting utterly demolished by the opposition. At one point during the game, his head turned instinctively to look at the scoreboard—it didn't matter what it even said at that point—and he realized something: He couldn't see it.

Not being able to see a 1940 Phillies game score reads more like a miracle than a curse, but Prothro turned to Heinie Mueller, or at least the vague outline of a figure he presumed to be Heinie Mueller.

"Heinie, can you see the scoreboard?" he asked.

"Sure, I can see the scoreboard," Mueller replied. "You don't think I've suddenly gone blind, do you?"

"No," Prothro said. "But I think I have."

The next day, his vision returned and an eye doctor had told him he was fine.

"I guess I got so dizzy watching the dizzy performance that my players were giving that I went partly blind," Prothro explained, an ambiguous and alarming prognosis, which carried no actual medical insight. "It affects you like that," Prothro said of the Phillies' particular style of last-place baseball.[2]

By June 15, 1941, with their lineup not hitting and pitchers constantly walking and their manager occasionally losing the use of his faculties, it actually seemed like the *perfect* time for Podgajny to give up: to just lay his glove down on the mound, give his manager a wave, and walk off the field with his head held high. Giving up would bring shame, sure, but putting on a Phillies uniform in the late '30s and early '40s was pretty embarrassing, too.

So. Giving up had its appeal.

It was the right time for an older teammate to talk him down.

But Podgajny, his big head deflated and his ego spilling out of his guts, didn't hear May say, "Don't give up."

He heard him say something else.

What it was Podgajny thought he heard was known only to Podgajny. When a man's blood is up, it only matters what he *thinks* was said. And a lot of times, when he's in that state, he's going to hear a lot said that isn't.

"I misunderstood him," Podgajny said years later.

As with many misunderstandings, the direct result was physical violence. Podgajny lunged for a very confused May's neck.

"Only the immediate intervention of teammates prevented possible bloodshed," he would later recall.[3]

They got their fists up, the universal symbol for shit about to go down, but before anybody could take a wild, 1940s-style swing, the fracas was suppressed by teammates and umpires. But you couldn't blame anybody—May had just been trying to support his pitcher, and Podgajny had naturally tried to strangle him.

Up in the Bronx that day, Joe DiMaggio hit his 13th home run of the season to help the Yankees win their seventh straight. But at Shibe Park in Philly, the Phillies also had a successful day when they were able to talk their young pitcher out of killing their third baseman right there in the field—even though Doc Prothro was going to fine that boy into oblivion.

Fans and writers followed DiMaggio from town to town all summer, eager to learn of his feats and miracles, thrilled by the suspense of his pursuit. Those tragically assigned to monitor the Phillies did so as morbidly curious observers, fascinated by the atrocity occurring in front of them, like a train derailment with hot dog vendors.

One newspaper ran a story on pitchers who had thrown one-hitters so far in the 1941 season, sympathizing with the pitchers who'd dominated but had their days ruined by a single knock. Tommy Hughes was one of them. The rest of the one-hitters on the list had come *against* the Phillies.[4]

Giving up is easy. So easy, in fact, that when it enters your head as an option, it's hard to get it to leave.

It's not that you don't give up because someone tells you to. You have to feel like you *can't*. You have to see that you're in the thick of it, but it's not always going to be like this. It's going to change, it's going to be different, *you're* going to be different, in ways you already are but haven't realized or grown into. You don't give up because you have more to do. You're getting somewhere, even if you don't know where you're going.

Or at the very least … you've already got the uniform on. Might as well finish the game.

Let the other writers and players spend the summer with DiMaggio. Everyone knew the real story was with the Phillies, who were routinely humiliated by other teams, by their own team, or by acts of a god who clearly hated them. A team on which a simple, quiet plea of support from one teammate to another would be met by attempted murder.

Johnny Podgajny would be talked down, return to the mound, walk the bases loaded, and somehow get out of the inning without further damage.

On the way back to the dugout, he and May shook hands, because it was only June and there was a lot of baseball left to play.

Can't give up now.

The next day, the sporting world had something other than Joe DiMaggio to look at. The streets of New York filled with would-be spectators of the Joe Louis-Billy Conn boxing match on Broadway.

Cy Peterman wrote in the *Inquirer* the crowds brought in by the fight were "in the most exciting fashion since the last Nazi invasion."[5]

It was shoulder-to-shoulder traffic on the streets, with everyone asking who you were picking or if you had any seats in the first five rows.

But getting a good ticket "was about as likely as for the Phillies to win a pennant," wrote Sid Feder in the *Inquirer*.[6]

Catching strays in a national sports story was pretty close to the spotlight for these Phillies. They'd just been shut out in two straight games (and four of their last five) before pulling out a victory in a game with almost no attempted stranglings. If it weren't for that five-game losing streak in the middle of the month, they'd have had a winning record in June!

Podgajny's gutsy win over the Cubs in game two of their June 15 doubleheader may have bought this team a little good press. But that all disappeared in the last game of their four-game set with the Cubs. With the nation's two sports stories—the boxing match and DiMaggio—happening in or at least close to New York City, sports fans in the Chicago metropolitan area had no choice but to settle for the Cubs playing the Phillies.

What Cubs fans saw was their own first baseman, Babe Dahlgren, put on a show. He handled 12 chances at his position perfectly, including three double plays—two of which included outs at home plate. Dahlgren threw in a hit and two walks and the Phillies had no real response, losing 3-1. Then one of their minor league managers quit.

DiMaggio hit a worthless double and neither scored nor knocked in any runs in the Yankees' game against Cleveland. Despite the innocuousness of his hit, it was his 29th game in a row with one.

Today, Yankees fans were mad at him for what he *hadn't* done. What kind of ballplayer doesn't do something the game has never seen before as soon as possible? *Where was this last year?* folks wondered. In 1940, the Yankees hadn't won the American League pennant for the fifth year in a row, but a 29-game hit streak probably would have helped. DiMaggio had missed the beginning of the 1940 season, and in fact, despite being with the Yankees since 1935, he had yet to play a full season, one writer pointed out. Though he did still win his second consecutive batting title.

After 55 games in 1940, the Yankees had been 6.5 games out of first place. This year, with DiMaggio barreling toward history, and having beaten Cleveland, 6-4? They were only one game out.

Can't give up now.

June 17–19

The sports world turned away from DiMaggio for a moment to fully face the boxing ring in mid-June. Billy Conn was expecting to *survive* his fight with Joe Louis. The lead story on the front of most sports sections on June 17 had at least something to do with their upcoming bout. But Conn had found something more than just a title card: He'd found love, and planned to marry his sweetheart as soon as possible.

Perhaps too soon. This wasn't just *any* fiancée. This was Mary Louise Smith, daughter of former Phillies player Jimmy Smith.

Jimmy Smith was famous for two things, both having occurred in 1921: hitting a home run off Grover Cleveland Alexander, and being arrested by a cop on horseback for beating up a guy who walked in front of a car full of Phillies players. The shouting match that had preceded the assault was full of "remarks that reflected on the pedestrians' ancestry" made by the Phillies players.[1]

It was commonly known that when Jimmy Smith said he was going to hit you, he was probably going to hit you (unless he was handcuffed or you were chasing him on horseback). But at retirement age in 1941, with his daughter trying to marry a *boxer* and all, you'd assume he'd think twice about throwing a fist at his future son-in-law.

Instead, when informed that Conn and his daughter had secured a marriage license, the former Phillies infielder announced, "I'll punch the hell out of that Conn if he marries my daughter—and he's the first to admit I can do it!"[2]

That's a lot of confidence for a .219 hitter, and certainly a greater amount of confidence than that which traveled with the current Phillies.

By June 17, the 1941 Phillies were adrift on the endless grasslands, coasting across the Midwest from Chicago to St. Louis, the hum and sputter of a bus engine in their ears as they rode from letdown to letdown.

The midwestern road trip was scheduled to last 23 days. The Phillies made it longer by only winning four games from June 14 to July 4. From June 17-19, they played three of them against the Cardinals and couldn't find a win.

Boom-Boom Beck retired no batters in game one, a performance that exists only in theory and, upon the deaths of all who witnessed it, will be appropriately lost to time. Prothro sent Frank Hoerst out next and the Cardinals just bashed him, too. Prothro was done waving at the bullpen for the day, he decided, and just left Hoerst out there, perhaps even dipping out at one point to have a smoke and a Coke or four. No one could blame him.

Hoerst was on the mound for five and a third innings, giving up most of the Cardinals' hits and runs that day, but he did have the most strikeouts of any Phillies pitcher in the game (2).

The Dodgers beat the Cubs up in Brooklyn, so the Cardinals were motivated to beat the Phils and keep their lead over rest of the National League. And against the Phillies, they could settle for being only half-motivated.

The Cardinals' starter, Mort Cooper, allowed only six hits, while that Phillies trio of Beck-Hoerst-and-Rube Melton got lit up by anybody with a bird on their shirt, giving up an 11-3 loss.

The Phillies would have no problem scoring against the Cardinals on June 18, however. With Cardinals starter Max Lanier on the mound, they slapped together a late rally out of some spare offense St. Louis had left lying around.

Two walks with one out in the eighth gave the opportunity to Bobby Bragan to single in a run, and with two outs, Johnny Rizzo knocked in two more with a bases-loaded single. And just like that, the Phillies had not only equaled their run total from the previous day, but ended Lanier's 21-inning shutout streak.

Unfortunately, they were down 7-0 when their little rally had started, and it was still 7-3 at the end of the game. The message from the Cardinals to the 500 American soldiers in attendance was clear: The absence of mercy *assures* victory.[3]

Sports seemed to be teaching that lesson a lot lately. The previous night, handsome Billy Conn had learned it when he'd missed Joe Louis with a left hook, giving Louis the only window he'd needed to atomize Conn's jaw with a right cross. Then he unloaded a storm of punches into Conn, ultimately beating Jimmy Smith's son-in-law into submission before Smith would get the chance to do so himself.

From a massage table after the fight, Louis would claim he'd known Conn was going to "miss [and] then lose his head," leading to an easy victory. Then he laughed.[4]

Fortunately for Conn, he didn't have a ball game to play the next day and could lick his wounds in secret. The Phillies never had that option. They had a 5-2 lead on June 19 before the score was tied, untied, tied, untied, tied, and then untied by a game-winning walk-off single that the Phillies did *not* hit, causing them to lose, 7-6.[5]

The Cardinals' biggest problem in 1941 was that they couldn't hold onto first place. The Phillies' biggest problem was that they were losing faster than Joe DiMaggio could make history.

"Something is always happening to the Phillies and usually it's a defeat," read the *St. Louis Dispatch* on June 20.

All summer, everyone saved their best lines for the Phillies. Their intense last-placedness made them a muse for wisecrackers, joke smiths, and quipsters from coast to coast. The lofty, mythical tones with which writers described DiMaggio's achievements—when they weren't in the mood to tear him down—were balanced by the snide remarks and casual jabs at the lousiest team in the game.

But there were times, like in late June, when writers could only speak with head-shaking bewilderment after what they'd witnessed at a Phillies game.

"Sometimes defeat comes in the early innings," the *Dispatch* said about the Phillies. "Then again it might be right in the middle of the game, or in the waning moments of battle with victory so near at hand. A base on balls here, a pop hit there, a bounder through the infield, a looper over an infielder's head. Those are the troubles of the Phillies, who actually have suffered more defeats than the Browns, but whose only consolation, perhaps, is that they haven't so many stockholders."[6]

The subject of such perplexed prose was the Phillies' loss to the Cardinals on June 19, when they'd built a 2-0 lead thanks to some early shenanigans from St. Louis (a throwing error and a wild pitch, or as the Phillies would have called it, "a rally").

They'd immediately let the Cardinals back in the game, but got home runs from Stan Benjamin and Johnny Rizzo to make it 5-2. Five straight Cardinals singles—including a two-run back breaker from Johnny Mize, playing in his first game since Memorial Day weekend—and a sac fly had knotted the score in the sixth, but Rizzo slapped a sac fly to give the Phillies one of those late one-run leads that everyone knew they wouldn't hold.

And they didn't.

After Frank "Lefty" Hoerst allowed a runner to reach second with one out, Doc Prothro brought in Tommy Hughes to end the game. With a runner on second base in the ninth and the Phillies up 6-5, Cardinals second baseman Frank Crespi drove Hughes' pitch straight into the ground. The ground, in turn, tried to send it back to the sky, the ball catching such a high and favorable bounce that Crespi reached base safely despite the ball ultimately landing in Hoerst's glove, several feet from where it had been hit.

As usual, this stupid moment was followed by an even more stupid one, as Cardinals late-game defensive substitute Steve Mesner cracked a sac fly that sent the game into extras.

Hughes stayed on the mound into the eleventh and Crespi swatted another of his offerings into the dirt. Once more there was a lucky bounce, this time over second base. It was the Cardinals' 16th one-run victory of the season, solidifying them as baseball's most annoying opponent and the team least affected by gravity.

Hughes hit the showers. At least he didn't have to get up early for class.

One St. Louis newspaper called the Phillies "hopeless," and compared the team to "the man who bit the dog." They even suggested a new nickname, "Doc Prothro's problem boys," a name focused more on accuracy than cleverness.[7]

"Because the Phillies are the Phillies, the Redbirds, for the first time this year, have been able to maintain a three-game first-place margin for more than 24 hours," read the *Post-Dispatch*.

The 1941 Phillies may have been unsuccessful at just about every aspect of the sport they played, but consider this—sometimes, they weren't playing baseball. Hell, sometimes, they weren't even awake! And you can't be the worst team in baseball when you're asleep.

"You can laugh at the Phillies," wrote in one reader to the *Inquirer*, "but I'd like to be able to go to sleep every night with as clear a conscience as old Cy Blanton."[8]

And where was Joe DiMaggio in all of this? It was his job to make baseball look good after the Phillies made it look impossible.

But DiMaggio was blowing it, too. He made a bad throw to give the Giants a first-inning lead. Typical DiMaggio, always starting to wilt when the pressure gets—oh no, sorry. That was *Vince* DiMaggio on the Pirates overthrowing the cut-off man. On June 19, *Joe* DiMaggio went 3-for-3 with a home run and a walk against the White Sox. Hell, he basically went 4-for-4, since Tommy Henrich hit a triple with his bat, too.

They were starting to talk a lot louder about this DiMaggio hit streak that was going on. He'd crossed the 30-consecutive-games milestone in the last couple of days and finally the conversation had gone from how he wasn't doing enough to how he might be doing something no one else had ever done.

The papers noted how Rogers Hornsby had the National League record of 33 consecutive games with hits, which DiMaggio was about to overtake. George Sisler held the modern hit streak record at 41 games. "Wee" Willie Keeler had the overall record with 44, Ty Cobb once had a hit streak reach 40 in 1911. And when they start listing your contemporaries and they say "Ty Cobb," you know you're probably headed for the record books. The nation's eyes were open to DiMaggio's accomplishment, and they knew they were watching history.[9]

The Yankees, however, were struggling, thankfully managing to "[find] their way back to the victory trail," by beating the White Sox, 7-2.[10]

Yes, after wandering the desert of a losing streak that had reached an unconscionable *two games*, the Yankees were finally *back*, and a grateful nation breathed a sigh of relief. Meanwhile, the Phillies packed up in St. Louis and headed back out across the plains up to Pittsburgh, knowing full well that they were on a journey from which there was no return; only waiting for whoever was going to take a swing at them next.

June 20–22

A photo of Ike Pearson appeared in the December 1942 issue of *The Marine Recruiter*, showing him just before he shipped off for training at Quantico. The magazine boasted that their boy Pearson, a "lean chucker," was a big-league pitcher, then went out of their way to mention his team as the "last-place Phillies."

It was probably a mistake to let the Marines know the 1941 Phillies existed, as they wanted only the most inspirational American success stories in their heads to motivate them into charging a machine gun nest. If the Marines were told that the 1941 Phillies were among the grateful Americans waiting for them when they got home, they'd have nothing to fight for.

"One of the most dependable pitchers on the Philadelphia Phillies," the magazine called Pearson. "Pearson should wind up an efficient grenade pitcher."

Picture it, won't you: Phillies reliever Ike Pearson, striding stealthily into enemy territory, armed only with a single hand grenade, carefully pulling the pin, going into his wind-up, while only 60 feet away, a sleeping German patrol …[1]

The war was tomorrow's problem. It was late June 1941, the Phillies were playing the Pirates, and Pearson had figured out how to blow up a ball game *without* using a grenade.

Nick Etten hit his eighth home run on June 20, a three-run shot that gave the Phillies a 6-2 lead. Their starter, Johnny Podgajny, ran out of juice somewhere in the seventh and Pearson was brought in after the Pirates had mounted a four-run punishment in response to the Phillies scaring up a little offense.

The 6-2 lead was smashed into a 6-6 tie going into the ninth, and with the Phillies playing on the road, you know where this was headed. Pearson walked Elbie Fletcher. Then he walked Vince DiMaggio. Then Virgil Davis.

With two outs, the Marines' leanest chucker was out of bases on which to hide his mistakes. Faced with the prospect of getting the game's last out, he found himself face to adolescent face with the Pirates' Frankie Gustine.

Gustine had arrived at spring training in 1940 and been set upon by the reporters who were utterly amused at the idea of a young person. At 20 years old, Gustine wasn't an outlier on a baseball field by any means. But still, "they often described [Gustine] as a 'boy,' or 'cherubic faced,' and jokingly made references to him not yet needing to shave."[2]

Now he was 21, and things were different. Yes, Gustine still maintained that youthful energy that makes young people want to "run everywhere" and "hope for things," but one *New York Times* writer had called him the "best second baseman in baseball." A debatable statement, but still, someone *had* said it.

This was a chance for Gustine, the man with a child's face, to prove how adult he was. Gustine came to the plate against Pearson, took the pacifier out of his mouth, and stepped in with the bases loaded and two outs. He lined a single to left field, Fletcher came in to score, the Pirates walked it off, and the Phillies traipsed off the field, beaten again, only this time by a child.

Good pitching is harder to find than mediocre pitching, which was closer to what Pearson offered throughout his four years in baseball before losing three seasons to the Marines.

But mediocre pitching beats bad pitching, because bad pitching is never around for very long. Or at least, it shouldn't be. The Dodgers believed this, as they were trying to make a deal to acquire some mediocre pitching.

Brooklyn Dodgers president Larry MacPhail was having trouble trying to get his outfielder Dixie Walker to play for nothing, so contract negotiations had devolved into resentful grumbling. MacPhail's next move, he determined, would be to send Walker packing and bring in some new player to yell at for wanting money.

MacPhail *really* wanted Hank Leiber from the Cubs. If that didn't work out, he'd take Johnny Rizzo from the Phillies—and if he made a deal with the Phillies, word was he'd get them to throw in Pearson as well. If they wouldn't take Walker, MacPhail reasoned, he'd try to swap in Luke Hamlin, a power hitter who wasn't power hitting very much lately.

"[MacPhail] has been a bit peeved, on and off, at Luckless Luke this year," wrote one sportswriter, "and currently the peeve is on."[3]

A trade with America's new favorite team could be just what the Phillies, a team whose peeve had been on or months, needed. At least for the attention.

In 1941, if you were talking baseball, you were talking DiMaggio, Ted Williams, or the surging Brooklyn Dodgers with Pete Reiser and Dolph Camilli and Pee Wee Reese and that Kirby Higbe—say, didn't he used to pitch for the Phillies? He sure does hate when people bring that up.

The Dodgers had been that famous squad of "Bums" who repeatedly let down their fans until one magical summer in 1941 when they would finally win the National League pennant but then have that same magical summer end the way *many* teams had since the beginning of baseball, with an ass-kicking by the Yankees.

The Phillies had neither Joe DiMaggio nor Ted Williams on the roster and were still very much in the "getting their ass kicked" part of being an underdog. But they had seemed to have entered a golden age of running into Joe DiMaggio's brother a lot.

As Kirby Higbe had learned, you never knew when your last day on the Phillies would be. You just knew it wouldn't be when you wanted it. Vince DiMaggio's RBI double in the third inning on June 21 helped bring in both the Pirates' runs, and Phillies starter Lee Grissom got exactly the amount of help he expected from his lineup (zero).

It was common practice by now to read a Phillies game recap and be told that the starting pitcher had fared quite well, or at least would have, had it not been for an outburst of catastrophic bullshit that ended with the other team in front. Their penchant for such moments, combined with their lineup's tragic incapacity for contact, contributed to the 22 times in which they were shut out (the Phillies shut out their opponents only four times in 1941).

It was also true that if an opposing pitcher had ever worn, touched, or even looked at a Phillies uniform in the past, it wouldn't be long after they joined another team that they got their heads right and rediscovered their fastball. Nothing made things make sense like leaving the Phillies.

Joe Bowman threw for the Pirates on June 21 and authored their 2-0 win. He was the return the Phillies had received in exchange for sending all-star shortstop Dick Bartell to the Giants in 1935, and the Giants regretted it. They offered $10,000 to buy Bowman back, but—presumably thrilled to see another team experience regret—Nugent hung onto him.

From 1935 to 1936, Bowman did his best for the Phils. His worst game was probably against the Reds on August 24, 1935, when he was "wild as a hawk" and gave up four runs, two walks, two hit batsmen, and eight runs in one third of an inning. The Phillies lost 13-2.

"A very pleasant afternoon," the *Cincinnati Enquirer* called it. "No protest made by anybody but the [Phillies] pitchers."[4]

At least back then, the Phillies had Hugh Mulcahy to send in and clean things up. In 1941, he was off god knows where, fighting for his country or whatever. Not exactly a team player.

By 1941, Bowman was a Pirate. His last game for the Phillies had been an 11-7 win in September 1936, in which his offense had finally figured out "run support" and scored seven times in one inning before immediately forgetting how to do it again. Bowman's need for revenge against his last team, whistling as it shoveled dirt on itself, likely stemmed from thoughts of "what might have been" after the Phillies had finally come through for him on his last day playing for them. Or maybe "what might have been" was more of a bad thing, and he viewed the Phillies as an evil that must be destroyed. Could've been either.

Out for revenge on June 21 or not, Bowman got it. The Phillies' starters were good for two hits. Joe Bowman's ERA went down to 2.59 on the season. Grissom wore the loss, and his reliever, Bill Crouch, was almost immediately traded to the Cardinals.[5]

Bowman could sit contentedly in the dugout the next day as the Phillies and Pirates played two, knowing they couldn't hurt him anymore.

The Phillies managed to win game two of the doubleheader, which ignited a spark of confidence in young Danny Litwhiler. He was becoming a breakout star with his undying enthusiasm and continued interest in baseball despite playing for the Phillies. He wouldn't abide a rude comment about his team, however, as it was the Phillies who'd found him on "baseball's bone pile" and given him a second chance.

While playing for the Tigers' Toledo affiliate in 1939, Litwhiler ran right into a fence and tore up the cartilage in one of his knees. Sent home, Litwhiler loitered about his hometown of Ringtown, Pennsylvania like some sort of shiftless townie. Dissatisfied with his shredded dreams, Litwhiler found a pen and paper and wrote to the only man who he believed could get him out of this jam: Gerald Nugent.

But Nugent needed more than stats to bring a player into the Phillies organization. He needed to see a low price tag. He needed to feel like he was getting a deal. He needed to think he couldn't lose. Money, that is.

Litwhiler's plan did all three. In his letter, he asked the Phillies to pay for surgery to fix his knee cartilage. After that, assuming it worked, he offered to play for the Phillies for free.

Nugent liked the sound of that—the word "free," I mean—and agreed to the deal that came to him in a stranger's letter. And that's how somebody could get a job playing Major League Baseball in the 1930s.

After his exciting end to the 1940 season, Litwhiler was back and ready to take off, dead set on making Nugent and Doc Prothro proud.

"I can hit this National League pitching as well as any other," Litwhiler told reporters. "As soon as it gets hot, you'll see the Phillies moving up—and I'll be going up with them."[6]

In the twin bill against the Pirates on June 22, Litwhiler went 6-for-10 with two doubles and a triple on the day, scored four runs and knocked in one, making him partially responsible for five of the eight runs the Phillies scored.

And yet, he was not listed among the stars of the day. That honor went to guys like his teammate Nick Etten, who was solid at the plate, and also Joe DiMaggio, who had hit a home run in the sixth to give the Yankees a record-breaking 18 games in a row with a round-tripper. But even more staggering was DiMaggio's 35 straight games with a hit, *and* the fact that the Yankees had beaten the Tigers, 5-4, in the bottom of the ninth on a bases-loaded walk after a rally started by … Joe DiMaggio.

As objective professionals, the writers couldn't literally throw roses at DiMaggio, so they did the *professional* thing and used their words.

"From the shores of the Harlem all the way to the banks of the gorgeous Gowanus in Brooklyn, the folks who go in for the sport of hit-and-run were giving out with Hoop-la and hurrah over the jobs their heroes did Sunday," read one story, using a breathtaking amount of syllables to construct the DiMaggio legend.[7]

The Phillies left Pittsburgh with one win out of four tries and hit the road to Cincinnati. As they left town, Nugent, who was becoming a real wheeler and dealer, sold 23-year-old Roy Bruner to the International League's Rochester club for an undisclosed amount.

Bruner was another young hurler that Prothro just didn't want to have to think about. He'd mentioned during spring training in 1940 that with a bit more stamina, Bruner and Ike Pearson could be effective, but "Gosh darn it, I'm not worried about my pitchers," Prothro had ranted. "What I need is a couple players who can give me a long hit occasionally and drive in some runs."[8]

What Doc needed was *both*, preferably, and he didn't really get either. The 40 runs Bruner had earned in 19 games for the Phillies since 1939 were the only ones he'd get to give up in the majors. When Nugent traded him, Bruner hadn't pitched in a game for two weeks. But a few more dollars slid back in Nugent's direction, so with that, and the Phillies win (but mostly that) everybody was happy.

Except Bruner, who, in addition to getting sold back to the minors, had also received notice from his local draft board.[9]

June 24–26

Boom-Boom Beck's start on June 24, 1941, went a long way toward explaining why the Phillies only won two of the 34 games in which he appeared that year. And it wasn't just because of him.

By now, the name "Phillies" appearing in a newspaper was almost always preempted by the words "last-place" or "lowly," as if the audience would forget who they were.

The Reds beat the Phillies last night.

The who?

You know, the team from Philadelphia.

Never heard of them.

Really? You don't know the last-place Phillies?

Oh, you mean those lowly Phillies!

Yes, the pathetic Phillies, who are truly awful. The common, baseborn, ignoble Phillies.

Got it. So what about th—

The toxic, vile, stinking Phils; those wretched boys from between the rivers. Awful and incompetent. They'll try to kick your dog and miss.

Right—

Those drooling, boneheaded plebeians unworthy of walking in daylight. Back to the sewers, I say, you subhuman garbage!

Honestly, I don't even like baseball.

And why would you?! Because of the Phillies, I mean.

And so on.

Their ineptitude was more than synonymous with them. It was basically a part of their name. By June 24, whatever luck they'd had against the Reds thus far was gone, too, meaning they'd lost the favor of the last baseball god and now floated agnostically in last place.

Beck weaponized his looping curve as best he could and mixed in some off-speed stuff to keep Cincinnati from hitting anything too hard. This plan worked for three innings. Frank Hoerst replaced Beck in the eighth and continued his stretch of dominance, allowing two runs and watching Joe Marty commit a two-base error in the outfield, presumably as the sounds of screaming inside Hoerst's head got louder and louder.

The Phillies' offense clobbered the ball straight into four double plays. Bucky Walters had started for Cincinnati and got off to a typical slow start, but even then, the Phillies failed to score until the ninth inning and needed the gift of two consecutive infield errors by the Reds to push a run across.

Some might say the difference between a 5-0 loss and a 5-1 loss is the dignity of that run.

But.

"The slow-moving Phils were just so many pushovers to Bucky," read the *Cincinnati Enquirer*.

There was little more to do when writing descriptions of the Phillies than insult them. Based on their level of play, it still technically counted as objective coverage.[1]

Across the league, baseball's youth movement was underway. The Phillies were, despite their record, a great example. Young players like Tommy Hughes (21), Danny Litwhiler (24), Johnny Podgajny (21), and Bobby Bragan (23) were occasionally highlighted in the press for their potential in the years ahead based on the skill they'd already shown. Hughes was lauded as an NL Rookie of the Year contender. A 15-year-old from Litwhiler's hometown found the slugger so inspiring that he was on his way to Syracuse to try out for the International League.[2] As bad as they were, not even the Phillies could stop *every* kid from loving baseball.

Nick Etten, though basically geriatric at 27 years old, was also an intriguing figure for those who covered the sport. He'd played for the Athletics before dipping back down to the minors, where an impressive season with the Orioles had brought him to the attention of the Phillies. As the summer pushed onward and outmatched rookies packed their bags, only those who'd figured out how to adjust to big-league pitching remained.

Etten was one of them (technically). He was big and strong. He had poise. He played multiple positions (outfield and first base). He was hitting over .300 and slugging over .500. And, most importantly to Philadelphia area fans, he was from the Philadelphia area.

"Philadelphia fans have a warm spot in their hearts for Etten because they can recall him as a star on the Villanova college team a few years back," read one paper.

"One of the best of the current freshman crop!!" read a comic illustration of Etten early in his playing career. In one of the images, he was fielding a grounder and saying, "I'll make one of the Philadelphia teams yet!"[3]

The most crucial part, of course, was that the Phillies had been able to put Etten in their lineup while only paying him $10,000.

In the ensuing doubleheader the Phillies and Reds played on June 25, Etten hit three singles, the offense's special of the day. The Phillies had 11 hits, all singles, in game one, losing 8-3, but Danny Litwhiler began a hit streak of 10 games, and a stretch in which he'd hit in 26 out of 27. His home run in game two was the Phillies' only non-single hit of the day.

Philadelphia Phillie Nick Etten kneeling in front of the screen at Braves Field. (Courtesy of the Boston Public Library, Leslie Jones Collection)

There seemed to be a DiMaggio inside of Litwhiler, straining to get out but suppressed by his inconsistency, luck, and being on the Phillies, who of course lost game two as well, 5-1.

It was a loss that had started with the Phillies' Lee Grissom throwing six innings of no-hit ball, but the Reds still finding a way to score on him twice—or, more accurately, being given ways to score on him by Grissom's teammates. Johnny Rizzo had a hell of a day at third, messing up two plays in the fourth, one of which led to two runs scoring and the other probably doing the same if Phillies catcher Bennie Warren hadn't gunned down a would-be base stealer for the third out.

Doing the best he possibly could still wasn't enough to keep the Reds off the board, it seemed, and so in the seventh, Grissom shut it down. When Stan Benjamin forgot he had sunglasses and lost a pop-up in the sun, "Grissom appeared to give up right there," said one writer, and the Reds added three more runs.[4]

The Reds felt so hot that when they left for their next series in St. Louis, they scheduled an exhibition game against a minor league club in Kansas City on their off day. It was the first time all season that they had won a series against the "gentlemen at the bottom of the National League," robbing the Phillies of one of their few brag-worthy accomplishments. The Reds were back to considering the Phillies lower than dirt. One write-up made sure to remind people that sweeping the Phillies was more of a chore than a challenge.[5]

It's not like this was new information; everybody could see the standings. It was June 25 and they were 26 games out of first place. The Phillies would still play 69 games before they won their 20th.

The knives of both critics and gods were coming out. The *St. Louis Dispatch* chose this moment to say, apropos of nothing, that the Phillies had the second-worst public address announcer in the league. Rumors had started that the Phillies were looking to jettison Doc Prothro and start over with another poor sap. A week after Mother's Day, Danny Litwhiler left the team to be with his mom as she had a gall bladder operation performed by the team physician. The mother of Hans Lobert, one of the Phillies' coaches, died.[6]

To make matters worse for any baseball fans who'd witnessed the Phillies try to play the sport they loved, something that mattered was also happening: Joe DiMaggio was about to lose his hit streak.

It felt like the Yankees were banging homers off the Browns all day on June 24, but none of them had come off the bat of DiMaggio. All DiMaggio had managed to do was ground-out, foul-out, and ground into a double play. The Yankee Clipper, at a mere 35 straight games with a hit, was about to whiff himself right out of history.

Henrich homered in the eighth to give the Yankees a 6-0 lead. The pressure was off DiMaggio, except for the fact that his next at-bat was his last chance to keep America from collapsing. Fortunately, DiMaggio had recently given an interview instructing hitters how to break out of a slump, and for Joe DiMaggio in 1941, going 0-for-3 in a game that was currently happening was as close to a slump as he could get. All he had to do was take his own advice.

It all came down to the toes, he said. DiMaggio recalled the struggles he'd endured before May 15, when his batting average dropped below .300 for the first time and America had entered its darkest days. People told him his step was too long, or his swing was too high. DiMaggio would swing through a pitch and some spectator sitting hundreds of feet away always had the reason.

But it wasn't until DiMaggio was batting on May 15 when the words of Lefty O'Doul echoed through his head: *"Keep that left toe pointed toward the pitcher and you'll hit to all fields."*[7]

With a slow rotation of his ankle, DiMaggio now pointed his toes threateningly at every pitcher, and it had been working for 35 straight games. The key to hitting, he said, other than the toe thing, was to simply not swing at bad pitches.

Whoever was supposed to teach the Phillies this had failed.

DiMaggio had, for a long time, a bad habit of swinging at junk outside of the zone, and what had it gotten him? Well, DiMaggio mentioned off-handedly, it had gotten him a 61-game hit streak with San Francisco in his first year of pro ball. But other than *that*, what had it gotten him? Nothing. Now, with more experience and a full set of toes, DiMaggio had become unstoppable.[8]

On June 24, down to his last hacks, DiMaggio brought his 0-for-3 bat to the plate, pointed his toes at Bob Muncrief of the Browns, and whacked a single to right.

The streak—and frankly, America—were saved.

The next day, DiMaggio flew out in his first at-bat, and by his second, the crowd was already in a frenzy; restless to see him notch number 37, and already tired of seeing him *not* do that. He rewarded them with a home run on the first pitch of the at-bat, and the Yankees won, taking the lead in the American League standings.

In the finale against the Browns, things got even hairier. DiMaggio's toes were really pointing that day and he was making a lot of solid contact: a 400-foot fly ball, a hard-hit liner, and a smashed grounder; but in each case, they either landed in a mitt or foul territory. The crowd was apoplectic. *This* was how it would end? Against the *Browns*?! The *Phillies* of the American League?!?

When the ninth came around, somebody else would have to get on base for DiMaggio to even have a shot at number 38. Red Rolfe was the hero who worked a walk, and Tommy Henrich obliged the superstar by bunting Rolfe over to second, taking a double play off the board. DiMaggio came up and knocked in Rolfe with a double.[9]

The long waits didn't hurt his public admiration. One writer, casting the lineups for the MLB All-Star Game, slotted in DiMaggio to every position for the American League except catcher, saying that, under this system, DiMaggio would get to position himself anywhere he wanted on the diamond at any point. All the pitchers could throw spitballs or shine balls to their heart's content and even take a nail file out to the mound. This would require, the writer said, a change in the rules by Commissioner Kenesaw Mountain Landis, but if Landis didn't acquiesce, the writer suggested that he would be fined $26,000,000.[10]

A picture of DiMaggio lounging in a chair while being fed by his pregnant wife, Dorothy, was run in one paper above a story in which he was referred to as "the perfect ballplayer." Somehow, the quiet California boy sprung an ego.

"Joseph Paul DiMaggio III will always be able to say he was born the year I set the record," DiMaggio told reporters. "That'll make it easier for folks to remember his birthday."

"Suppose it's a girl?" a reporter asked.

Same, DiMaggio said. Except it'd be "Josephine."[11]

June 27–29

The Phillies also lost in a walk-off the next night against the Pirates, also by a score of 7-6. They would lose seven of eight going into June 27, and then they would lose eight of nine, but also lose something even worse than the game.

All in all, June 27 was a regular evening for the Phillies: Intense summer heat radiated off the field. The Giants beat them, as they would in 16 out of 22 tries all year. Tommy Hughes started the game but had the same kind of luck as when he'd ended one the week before.

Hughes got no outs, allowing two walks and a single, and Doc Prothro, well aware of where things were headed, yanked him in favor of Si Johnson. The papers were back to pointing and laughing, focusing not on Hughes' performance in the game itself, but rather a story about him getting too much mud in his cleats earlier that season in Chicago and falling off the mound during his delivery.

"He put the spin on himself instead of the ball!" snickered the write-up.[1]

Hughes failing to record an out against the Giants seemed like the disaster of the day for the Phillies, until a face-strikingly poor moment occurred in the fourth.

Danny Litwhiler and Joe Marty got themselves on base in the first, and if there was one guy in the 1941 Phillies lineup they wanted runners on base for, it was Nick Etten. He was hitting .319 and slugging .522 and generating a lot of the offense that went to waste when the Phillies lost their games. He came up in the first and clocked a three-run shot off the Giants' Bill Lohrman to deliver a 3-0 lead for the Phillies.

By the fourth, a bunch of other things had happened, the sum of which was that the Phillies had lost their lead and were now down 7-4.

Johnny Rucker led off for the Giants and punched a grounder to short. Etten, playing first, received the throw just as his jaw received Rucker's elbow. He spun, fell, and when the dust settled, he was lying unconscious on the field, "… out colder than a guy who had walked into Joe Louis' Sunday punch."[2]

An umpire bent over and gave Etten's still body a quick look, trying to determine if the Phillies had finally been so bad that it had killed someone. Etten was still breathing, however, and they managed to heave his 200-pound body onto a stretcher and get him somewhere safe, away from the Phillies.[3]

The good news later was that Etten's jaw wasn't broken. But he was suffering from a "badly wrenched" neck, so his doctors decided that he was better off in the hospital and not with his team. Baseball experts agreed.[4]

For some reason, this game was Gerald Nugent's breaking point. He'd seen plenty of losses, three straight last-place finishes, and a mountain of players' bodies pile up over the years, but this game, this loss, and this team finally made the Phillies' president say enough was enough.

"I have all the patience and indulgence anyone could ask for," Nugent told reporters. "But there is a limit to it and I've just about reached that point. There are going to be some changes made—just as soon as we can get replacements."[5]

Nugent said they'd hoped the team's veterans would guide and support the young core. That didn't really happen, so it was time to tell the players that their jobs were already lost and that the Phillies were simply waiting for the next suckers they could find to take their spots. Just as soon as Nugent felt like paying for better players. Or at least, *other* ones.

Word was Rogers Hornsby was coming to town to whip the Phillies into shape as their new manager. Hornsby, famous for never drinking or smoking or carousing around town with ladies or even going to the movies out of fear it would hurt his eyesight (but boy did he rack up some gambling debt), was sure to bring his trademark looseness to the Phillies clubhouse that would in turn bring out the best in them. Nugent denied it.

"Nugent said he knew nothing about reports that Rogers Hornsby, former major league manager, would succeed Doc Prothro as manager," read the story.

"'You can't blame Doc,' Nugent said. 'No manager can go up there and bat for his men.'"

While the Phillies were up in New York, DiMaggio was in their house, getting on base four times against the A's at Shibe Park. To extend his hit streak to 39 games, he singled in his first at-bat, then homered a little later just to be safe. Now he was just two games short of Dick Sisler's 41-game hit streak, a milestone the *Brooklyn Eagle* said was meaningless; DiMaggio's hit streak was already better than Sisler's, they said, because it had more home runs.[6]

"Speaking of Joe DiMaggio," gushed one writer, "that boy has the best form of a baseball player ever witnessed by this writer. He literally looks the part of the so-called perfect baseball player both afield and at bat … We saw both the mighty Babe Ruth and Lou Gehrig perform with the Bronx Bombers, but it is our bet that after five more years, Joe DiMaggio will eclipse their performances, barring unforeseen accidents."[7]

Speaking of unforeseen events, Nick Etten eventually woke up in the hospital. In a more foreseen development, the Phillies would lose 13 of their next 15 games.

But not the *very* next one!

It took 12 innings, over three hours, and their starting catcher, but the Phillies beat the New York Giants on June 28, 1941, drinking messily from an oasis of glory in a desert of unwatchable nonsense.

"You would have thought the pennant were at stake," one writer mumbled after watching the Giants, in third place behind the Cardinals and Dodgers, play the Phillies, who were in eighth place behind everyone.[8]

It took until the eighth for the Phillies to make a ball game out of it, though the whole contest had been full of defense and pitching worthy of the postseason. Joe Marty was the hero, coming to the plate with the score 2-0 and Hal Marnie and Danny Litwhiler in scoring position. His single knocked them both in and tied the game, and the Phillies decided that this time, they were going to win it.

And this time, unlike other times they'd decided that, they actually did.

As they proceeded precariously into the ninth, the score knotted at 2-2, Tommy Hughes had replaced Cy Blanton—they'd split the 12-inning affair right down the middle and each pitched six frames. The Giants led off the ninth with a single, putting everybody on edge. When the next hitter took a close pitch the umpire called a ball. The write-up read like Bennie Warren just exploded:

"Warren flung the ball, his mask, his glove, and his chest protector in all different directions, and looked like he was going to throw [the umpire], too."[9]

After they swept up all the pieces of Bennie Warren, the at-bat would end with a line drive double play. The Phillies would hold off the Giants until a two-out single with runners on first and third by Stan Benjamin gave them the lead and Hughes went 1-2-3 on the Giants in the bottom of the 12th. Victory sealed.

They could get used to this, the Phillies thought—winning in New York, that is. Some guys do it all the time.

It seemed like every night, the sweet crack of lumber was echoing out of the parks blessed by DiMaggio. Because it was. The streak was a part of baseball now, almost separate from the guy maintaining it. If DiMaggio went 0-for-4 one night, the streak would be dead as dirt. But *he'd* be back in the lineup the next day.

Nothing else in the sport was even close to that impressive, not even the Yankees homering in 25 straight games or the Phillies not yelling at or punching each other anymore. Everything else was a footnote on the summer's most exciting non-military streak that made every Joe DiMaggio at-bat essential viewing.

There is very little in baseball that hasn't been done before, which is odd for a sport in which something new seems to happen pretty regularly. As change-makers arise, they are fighting against not just all of a baseball player's natural enemies—physics, luck, the other team cheating, etc.—but against all of history. As every record-chaser approaches a milestone, a ghost rises up to defend itself, and in this case, DiMaggio was approaching George Sisler's American League hit streak record of 41 games, set in 1922.

Fortunately, ghosts are terrible fighters. They can't talk and their translucent fists just go right through you. DiMaggio easily hit his way past Ty Cobb's 1911 hit streak of 40 games on June 28, with his next targets being Sisler's 41-game streak and Willie Keeler's 44-game salvo with which he'd opened the 1897 season.

But Sisler wasn't even a ghost yet, and wouldn't be for over 30 years. In fact, the next month, Sisler would be serving as the commissioner of the national semi-pro baseball tournament, set to take place that August in Wichita, Kansas. Sisler's first order of business was to ban a "magic-eye" technique meant to be used in place of human umpires. He was still of the belief that umps kept the game "red-blooded" rather than turning it over to a "light ray, designed to determine strikes at home plate by means of an electric beam."[10]

While Sisler protected the game from encroaching lasers, his appreciators arose in defense of his hit streak record. It's not inherently personal when a phenom starts knocking down old records, but as they get closer to each one, especially ones people thought would stand forever, there can be a sort of head-shaking offense taken, as though by surpassing a record, its previous holder is somehow eliminated from history. As hard as it can be to complete the feats that *make* history for someone like DiMaggio (though he didn't seem to be having too difficult a time with it), it can be even harder for those who've already *seen* history to accept that it's changing.

They'll find ways to remind you, as the record starts to topple, that the person who set it had to work harder for it, or had a bunch of disadvantages that today's players wouldn't have been able to handle, or deserves to keep it more than the new guy deserves to take it. We believe that the happiest moments we have watching baseball are the sport at its absolute peak, and anyone trying to climb to similar heights on another day, when we're at another age or in another mood, are … *wrong*, somehow.

But baseball is always changing. It's just very slow and hard to notice until we look around one day and all the names we used to know have been replaced by new names who want to make their *own* history, without any attachment to the players and teams formative to our fandom. People don't necessarily stand in the way of history, but they do like to call out as it passes them by—*Don't forget him. Don't forget* me.

"Few if any writers—and probably none of the readers—recall the sad aftermath of George Sisler's failure to hit in his forty-second straight game," wrote Harold Claasen. "It has been recalled as a day of despond ever since."[11]

Sisler had returned from injury with a 39-game hit streak and successfully hit in two more games before going hitless on September 18, 1922. According to his St. Louis Browns teammate, Pat Collins, Sisler was still injured when he came back, trying to hit one-handed in front of crowds so dense they brought in mounted policemen to maintain order.

As Sisler went for number 42, the Browns were playing the Yankees in a game with playoff implications. Sisler's day got more and more hitless as it went on, culminating in his final at-bat in the ninth with the Browns down 3-2.

"... his one good arm and his courage weren't enough," Claasen wrote.

The next year, Collins said, Sisler started having vision problems and was essentially playing with only one eye while still in his prime. Eventually, it was decided that this would impact his playing time.

This was the man DiMaggio was coming for: a one-armed, one-eyed champion who'd refused to put down his bat for as long as he could. You wouldn't want to blast that guy's hit streak record right out of his hands, would you Joe?

Joe did, immediately. With a double in game one of the Yankees' doubleheader against the Senators on June 29, he matched the 41-game AL record. With a single in the nightcap, he broke it. And he claimed he was only getting more powerful.

"It's up to the pitchers to stop me now," DiMaggio said. "The way I feel now, I don't believe I'll be my own undoing. The pressure's completely off now. I go to bat just as relaxed as if there never had been any streak."[12]

With a milestone being crushed in Washington, nobody was watching the Phillies—even more nobody than before.

Instead of a pair of solid starts on June 24, the Phillies and Giants pitching staffs portioned the contest into three- or four-inning microdoses of slop. The Philly papers said the Giants "outlasted and out staggered" the Phillies.[13] In another paper, the Phillies were mentioned in an article about how easy the Giants' upcoming schedule was.[14]

Ace Adams of the Giants was the first "Ace" in history to be named "Ace" by his parents and not get it as a nickname for being good at pitching or blowing Nazis out of the sky. Five years after this game, Adams would defect to the Mexican League for $50,000 and an apartment. He would play in a ballpark where the game occasionally stopped to let a train go through the outfield. He claimed he regretted nothing.[15]

Lee Grissom got the start and almost nothing else beyond it, retiring one batter before letting four runs stomp across the plate. Doc Prothro spit out his Coke in disgust, and sure, let's imagine him throwing the bottle at the wall, too. He yanked Grissom and sent out Rube Melton, then Si Johnson, then Ike Pearson, none of whom could stop the bleeding.

But the Phillies' offense came to play, briefly. They used a Johnny Rizzo homer and a cluster of fourth-inning singles to erase the Giants' early lead, then tacked on by pushing a base runner home with productive outs in the fifth and a Rizzo gapper in the ninth. The Phillies racked up seven runs, all of which would have come in handy had the Giants not scored 10. Ace Adams pitched the last four innings and got the win.

"Weird," one writer called it.

And there was still a whole other game to play.

"NO," bellowed the universe, and dumped a sky's worth of rain onto the field below. Everyone pretended to wait around for a little while before deciding they were all better off skipping the whole thing.

Rumors that Doc Prothro would be replaced were turning into more confidently shared rumors about Rogers Hornsby replacing him. In truth, Hornsby had just left a managing gig in Oklahoma City because the team sucked at both baseball and getting fans to come watch them play. Things got bad enough that the owner decided the $1,000 he was paying Hornsby was more valuable than having Hornsby around, and the timing of Hornsby's exit aligned perfectly with the rumors circulating about Prothro.[16]

The idea of coming to Philadelphia to manage the Phillies was appealing to no one. But the idea of coming to Philadelphia to *fix* the Phillies? Perhaps that would draw in the franchise's savior.

Hornsby was a baseball sheriff looking for a town to clean up. He could kick in the clubhouse doors, ban his new team from drinking and smoking, and tell them not to go to the movies anymore. He could whip them into shape or at least get them to come together as one against his draconian leadership. He would go from famous for a Hall of Fame career to famous for *two* Hall of Fame careers, as a player and a manager.

But Hornsby never came. Rumors were squashed here and there, but the idea of Hornsby riding in to save the Phillies made too much sense narratively for people to let it go. It wasn't until the end of the season, when fans looked around and saw that Prothro was still around, that they finally realized that Rogers Hornsby wasn't coming.

Nobody has ever forgotten Rogers Hornsby, George Sisler, or Joe DiMaggio, though perhaps they've lost the front of mindedness the stars enjoyed while playing baseball or still alive. But they have their names etched into respected baseball surfaces and shrieked by pundits trying to make a point. This, in baseball, confirms their status as icons, and no one can take that away, even by beating them. Or in some cases, at least trying to.

Les McCrabb pitched for the A's for a bit in the '40s. A catcher in Pennsylvania Amish Country told Connie Mack there was a kid out there who played a decent shortstop. Mack brought McCrabb in, threw with him, and told him he was a pitcher. Mack had a way of handing out fates. He was like God visiting you in a dream, only you were awake and He was wearing a straw hat (or a felt bowler if it was winter or early spring).

McCrabb got a little testy when he kept being used in games *and* batting practice and accused Mack of wearing him out. When his bad starts got worse, Mack accused him of not trying hard enough. This did not improve their relationship.[17]

In 1941, Connie Mack finally unleashed McCrabb on the American League, and McCrabb showed them the middling success that had strained his relationship with his boss. He made 23 starts that year with 11 complete games, but his most memorable start was made by somebody else.

The Yankees were coming to Shibe Park and they were whipping ass. Joe DiMaggio had a hit streak that hadn't ended in 39 games. But A's starter Johnny Babich had a plan. He'd beaten the Yankees five times in

1940, but it wasn't his turn in the rotation. So he talked McCrabb into trading starts with him so Babich could face the Yankees.

Babich bragged that he'd have DiMaggio down on strikes and then walk him the rest of the game to deny him his 40th straight game with a hit. You have never heard Johnny Babich's name before, so you have probably guessed that yes, DiMaggio easily doubled off of him in the third inning.[18]

Every challenger who stood in DiMaggio's way was obliterated by his swinging bat. All his opponents could do, they felt, was watch as his staggering success continued; and hope that they wouldn't be the ones to be forgotten.

Part Three: July

June 30–July 2

In time, there would be baseball scriptures written of the Brooklyn Dodgers' 1941 season as some of the purest, most narratively satisfying baseball ever played.

By the end of June, a million people had come to Ebbets Field to see the Dodgers so far in 1941 with only 70 games in the books; a million bodies through the turnstiles, paying to be tantalized by the city's scrappiest ballet. They wanted to see their working-class Brooklyn boys perform well enough to quiet all the *DiMaggio-talk* from across town; they wanted glory and pride brought to *their* side of the bridge; they wanted to see *their* team beat up on lost out-of-towners who wandered into the borough.

The 200 soldiers, the 6,000 children, and 1,000 orphans who were on hand to watch the Dodgers play the Phillies on June 30 wanted to see a vicious Brooklyn beatdown of the visitors. But some of them wanted a little bit more: something to take home with them.

The Dodgers did their job and beat the hell out of the Phillies. The game was not close. Dodgers fans were relaxed and enjoying the humiliation of the Phillies that they'd paid to see when a foul ball found its way from the diamond into the right-field boxes late in the game.

Everything changed.

Two fans went for it. Insults turned to jabs. Jabs turned to shoves. Shoves turned to poorly executed punches. And the next thing anybody knew, an usher and a cop showed up to separate the "two Tony Galentos," as reported by the *Daily News*, referencing a famed New Jersey boxer who once fought an octopus.[1]

The ejected parties missed a hell of a performance from Dodgers starter Whitlow Wyatt, who, beyond some annoying and meaningless home runs from Bennie Warren and Danny Litwhiler, had a pretty effortless day on the mound against the Phillies lineup, earning his 12th victory to lead the National League.

It was Johnny Podgajny's turn for the Phillies. He allowed six runs in four innings and hit the Dodgers catcher, Mickey Owen, in the head.

Owen was a 25-year-old backstop from a Missouri family of farmers and cops. As a minor leaguer in 1937, he famously told reporters while admiring his catcher's mitt, "That's the glove that's going to catch the next World Series for the Cardinals."

It took four years and a different team. And even then, with two outs in the ninth inning of game four of the 1941 World Series, Owen would, even more famously, use his mitt to drop a third strike and let the Yankees beat the Dodgers.

But all that suffering was in the future. On June 30, 1941, all Owen had to do was help the Dodgers beat the Phillies; a much simpler task, unless you've got a hole in your head.

It was the second inning when Owen stood in for the first time. Podgajny came inside with such a spin on the ball that it *kept* going inside. Owen pulled back and kept pulling back, but the ball just kept following him. It cracked him in the head over the left eye and he dropped to the ground, "a bloody, writhing heap in the dust of the batter's box."[2]

There probably wouldn't have been as much blood if the ball hadn't hit Owen right where he had been hit with a bat years before. The scar burst back open and the blood flowed, to the horror of fans and writers watching. Owen was unconscious for a few minutes but came to in the clubhouse before being put in an ambulance and taken to the hospital, where photographers got the obligatory shot of him with a bandaged head and his concerned wife leaning over him.

It seemed unlikely, with the gushing head wound and all, that Owen would be making the All-Star Game in Detroit, to which he'd been invited to play for the first time in his career. But he said he'd "try mighty hard to make it," assuming that slithery Johnny Podgajny wouldn't sneak into the hospital to finish the job.

The doctors explained that if the ball had been in a quarter-inch in any direction, it might have deflected off the bill of his cap, or possibly killed him. Who was to say? Head wounds weren't an *exact* science. But Owen didn't blame Podgajny; only himself, for not getting out of the way correctly enough.

Regardless of Owen's forgiving nature, he was the fifth Dodger who'd been beaned with a pitch in less than a calendar year, the *Daily News* stated. They weren't accusing anyone of anything. Just … putting it out there that they'd noticed.

With Owen safely hidden away from Podgajny, there was still a ball game to play, and the action resumed. The fifth inning, with Brooklyn up 3-0, saw another Dodgers rally, which included a grounder to Hal Marnie, who tried to catch the lead runner at second and help them escape another mess.

The ump called it an out, but because Bobby Bragan had caught the throw with his back to the official, the ump hadn't seen how he'd bobbled it. Umpiring at this stage of history had yet to account for "What if the players' backs are turned?" The third base ump had seen it all, however, and after a brief conference and some complaining by Leo Durocher, the call was reversed.

Doc Prothro wasn't having it. *You can't just* change *the* call. *It's* the call*! Why make calls at all if you're just going to change them?!*

But the umpires stuck to their guns, after totally reversing them of course, and after 10 minutes of screaming and hating everything, Prothro went back to the Phillies dugout with the bases still loaded.

Podgajny threw a wild pitch immediately. The Phillies lost 9-2. It was their 10th straight loss to the Dodgers.

A win, at this point, would be historic. More historic than, say, a man on his way to breaking George Sisler's 41-game hit streak?

No.

Word of the Phillies' next historic win was buried in their own sports section. As DiMaggio broke Sisler's record, the curmudgeons of the day released the final squeal of how things used to be with a plea not to forget Sisler as DiMaggio passed him by.

"We would like to apply the brakes for a moment and suggest you don't slough off George Sisler's deeds as just another busted record," Cy Peterman insisted in the *Inquirer*. "Sisler was one of our favorite athletes."[3]

Remember the summer of '22, Peterman asked his readers? When Sisler hit .420 while facing the best pitchers of the day who weren't handcuffed by all these "rules" about not throwing the ball at the batter's mouth? And he *still* hit safely in 41 straight games?

Peterman was performing an occasionally eye-rolling but important role: the sentry of time, watching it go by, and trumpeting what he had witnessed for posterity. Everybody lives in the present, but only a few names are remembered into the future. Peterman's column read like a plea from the past to not let Sisler be forgotten.

And beneath all that, all the record-breaking, honor-seizing, and legacy-upholding, buried under layers of ink and columns of numbers, one headline whispered from the bottom of the sports page: *Holy shit–The Phillies beat the Dodgers.*

A headline over the box score read, "YEP, ITS TRUE," as a Phillies win didn't even seem worth correcting a typo.

It hadn't been very long since the Dodgers *were* the Phillies. In his book *Baseball and Other Matters in 1941*, Robert W. Creamer wrote that before the glory days of the "Boys of Summer" Brooklyn Dodgers, the Dodgers "were simply awful, an inept team that disappointed its devoted fans year after year. The [Dodgers] were clowns ... and Brooklyn fans hungry for victory and the self-respect that victory brings would leave Ebbets Field after each embarrassing defeat muttering, 'Them bums. Them lousy bums.'"

Sure, "Bums" was what Peter Goldenbock would affectionately entitle his oral history of the Brooklyn Dodgers, but that was after they'd managed to crawl out of the sewer in the 1940s. The Phillies, frightened by the burn of daylight, watched them go, choosing to stay behind in the dark, wet slop.

In 1941, the Dodgers were on the brink of something better, and the Phillies were just a team they beat on the way there. But once in a while, the Phillies managed to land a soft punch.

"The Phillies today obtained some measure of revenge for indignities heaped upon them by the Brooklyn Dodgers by knocking Leo Durocher's ambitious warriors out of a tie for first place," read the story.[4]

Three hours in the heat of July was enough to break any pattern. "Fat" Freddie Fitzsimmons started for Brooklyn. The Phillies knocked him out in the second inning, and it was assumed that his poor performance could be accredited to the broiling July temperatures and his aforementioned fatness.

With the bases loaded in the tenth and no outs, Phillies outfielder Stan Benjamin whacked a grounder back at the drawn-in Dodger infield and managed to find space between third and short. Two Phillies runs came galloping in, breaking a 4-4 tie that had dragged the game into extras and delivering the Phillies a 6-4 victory. They had lost 18 of their last 21 games against Brooklyn.

The defeat meant more to the Dodgers than just the usual head-hanging shame for which losing to the Phillies required. Brooklyn was playing for something more than getting to take off their uniforms at the end of the day; they were fighting for what was known as "first place," and their loss to the Phillies let the Cardinals tie them for the National League's top spot.

The Phillies had perhaps heard rumors of a distant, fabled land called "first place" but otherwise had little to go on as to what it was or who was in it. Having recently unloaded another full clip into their own foot, some fans had begun to wonder if they were doing this on purpose. Perhaps, it was suggested, they were self-sabotaging so effectively that they could set an all-time low among full-season records.

But for the Phillies to be engaging in subterfuge of that kind, Cy Peterman wrote, they'd have to be *good* at something.

"From what we've seen of them on the basepaths," he wrote, "they couldn't catch up to a military secret on a motorcycle; as a squad they lack the instinct to surround it. The Phillies are oh, so slow."[5]

There was talk of a "vigilante band" being formed to teach the Phillies a lesson. But before any good Philadelphian could get their pitchforks still smeared with dried Redcoat blood out from under the floorboards, it was made clear that the "band" in question would be a literal musical band with the goal of serenading the Phillies with a rollicking rendition of "Get Out of Town." The gradual, Cole Porter-penned tune had been written for the musical *Leave it to Me!* and had a lengthy instrumental prelude before the lyrics began, which read today like a devastating series of owns.

At least the Dodgers had the All-Star Game to look forward to. The most surprising thing about six Dodgers making the 1941 NL All-Star team was that there weren't seven or eight. Kirby Higbe and Hugh Casey were left off but could have easily been used to strengthen the pitching staff, which boasted a litany of hurlers who'd humiliated the Phillies in 1941: Lou Warneke, Claude Passeau, Bucky Walters, Whit Wyatt.

And the victorious Phillies? Oh, don't you worry about them. Not only did they have their very own all-star, but they'd just picked up a stud second baseman from the minor league Houston Buffaloes, "the prize package in the Texas League."[6]

The Phillies had snuck Cy Blanton onto the all-star roster. The NL team's biggest weakness was said to be on offense, meaning that no Phillie would be the worst part of the team, as none of their hitters were good enough to be *on* the team. Therefore, they could submit a pitcher and actually be viewed as helpful to the cause. Take that, haters!

Then there was the kid the Phillies had found in the Texas League, Danny Murtaugh. During one stretch in May he went 15-for-33 with six doubles. The previous year he'd been second in hits and walks and third in stolen bases, and all Gerald Nugent had to give up for him was a presumably reasonable amount of cash and infielder George Jumonville.

And on top of all that for the Phillies, word got out that Merrill May was ambidextrous! That had to at least *double* his value! Who knew![7]

Baseball was entering a new era. Yes, Joe DiMaggio had the all-time hit streak record, sure, whatever. But the Phillies had beaten the Dodgers in a regular season game (the only kind of game they really played!) They had an all-star! They'd unearthed a *future* star—that's the best kind of star, the kind you don't have to pay much yet! Their third baseman had *two dominant hands*! What *wasn't* possible in a world like this?

"The Phillies have finally beaten Brooklyn," snorted Bob French in the *Inquirer*. "Now their main ambition is to win more games than pitcher Bob Feller."[8]

The next day, the Phillies had nine hits off Kirby Higbe and knocked him out of the game in the fourth. A genuinely mystified public watched as the Phillies played some uncharacteristically solid ball. And as anyone who's ever played a sport will tell you, the only thing easier than achieving success is sustaining it.

The Dodgers scored three runs off Phillies starter Frank Hoerst in the first inning, then two more off Boom-Boom Beck, also in the first inning. Rube Melton pitched the rest of the game. They scored on him, too. A lot. The AP said the Phillies were the Dodgers' "pet stooges."

So, as much as Cy Peterman feared the future, as much as the pages of history quickly faded and fell out of the book, as inevitable as the breaking of every pattern is over time, the Phillies were the Phillies, and they had plenty more losing to do.

They *did* win more games than Bob Feller.

It was kind of close though.

July 3–5

The day after America turned 165 years old, the *Inquirer's* daily limerick competition was a real doozy:[1]

> When the heat of the summer bears down,
> On all who must stay close to town.
> A cool bath is nice,
> Or a long drink with ice,

Submissions were open for a final line, but until the winner was selected, it would be yet another sense of incompleteness for a city on the edge.

The summer heat was present in more places than the unfinished child's poem. The Phillies had been feeling it bear down on them as well, and as they had showed up for work again on July 4, they had hoped for an ending as satisfying as the one missing from that limerick.

The fourth of July. One of many American holidays typically celebrated with explosions, accidentally and on purpose. But there were no fireworks for Joe DiMaggio on July 4, 1941. There was only a midsummer shower that scared the Yankees and Athletics off the field for a day.

The same universe that had used rain to wash away the soiled Phillies less than a week before now seemed to be gifting the Yankee Clipper with a day off to do his favorite non-baseball activities, which according to DiMaggio's many biographies included smoking and posing for photographs that would one day be used as book covers.

And so, Joe DiMaggio went home and waited. He'd hit safely in his 45th game in a row against the Red Sox two days prior. He had the new all-time record in consecutive games with a hit. There was nothing to do now but make insurance history.

The last time somebody in New York was setting an all-time streak, his name was Lou Gehrig. He'd died several weeks prior, and the Yankees had decided they wanted him back.

This time, he wouldn't be setting any records. Just hanging out by the centerfield flagpole, win or lose. The Yankees announced that Gehrig's statue at Yankee Stadium would be unveiled the day after America's birthday so as to not distract from the Yankees with all that Americanism, and the rain pushed that moment back a day, too.

DiMaggio's record-breaking hit had been a home run. They couldn't even find the ball. He signed the bat he'd hit it with and sent it to the San Francisco chapter of the USO to be auctioned off. Everything he touched while in a baseball game was now a future artifact to be gawked at by fans who'd yet to be born.[2] He was the man with the million-dollar DNA, well on his way to having his own set of iron eyes someday, immortalized in center field.

They may not have always played like it, but plenty of the 1941 Phillies have been immortalized, too. Danny Murtaugh would have his number retired by the Pirates. Nick Etten is in the Chicago Sports Hall of Fame and the Catholic League Hall of Fame. A descendant of his would become the first female coach for the Portland Sea Dogs.[3] Bobby Bragan is in the Alabama Sports Hall of Fame, the Texas Baseball Hall of Fame, and the Texas Sports Hall of Fame. When he was 87, he managed the Fort Worth Cats for a day, dethroning Connie Mack as the oldest manager in the history of professional baseball.[4]

And some haven't been. Johnny Podgajny would struggle to find work to support his wife and five children after baseball and died of a heart attack at 50.[5] Even immortality has its limits.

In another example of the universe's unending cruelty, DiMaggio may have gotten a day off on July 4 in 1941, but the Phillies had to play two games. It was clear they were in for it when the Braves' starter was announced: Manny Salvo, a man who hadn't won a start in his last 10 tries.

The last time Salvo had won a game had been the Braves' second game of the season. The offense spotted him three runs in the first that day and he shut down the opposing lineup, allowing only three hits, three walks, and one earned run. In the first eight frames, all he'd permitted was an infield single, keeping the hitters off-balance and off base.

Those hitters had also been the Phillies.[6]

On Independence Day, Si Johnson gave up RBI triples in back-to-back innings, and with Salvo on the mound, the Phillies managed almost nothing to counter them, losing 3-1. Then they pretty much forgot there was a second game about to start, which ended in a 2-0 loss. They had two hits. "They" is doing some heavy lifting in that description, as both hits were struck by only one Phillie, Merrill May. Did you hear that he was ambidextrous?

Losing had returned to Philadelphia. It had only been gone a day.

"The Phils took it on the chin twice here today before a slim crowd caused by scattering mid-day rain," read the grim lead in the *Inquirer*.[7]

The sense of loss drifted across the city and the people of Philadelphia had more than a couple of ball games taken from them. Belongings were left behind, dogs ran off, wrist watches went missing. A wire-haired mutt named Skippy disappeared near Overbrook. A purse full of cash was left behind in Wissinoming. A man in North Philly couldn't find his Smith & Wesson for the life of him, and the *Inquirer* helpfully published his home address in case anyone wanted to know where there was a house to rob with no gun in it.[8]

People were learning that their fates were intrinsically linked with the local nine whether they wanted them to be or not. And the bad times weren't even close to over, though you wouldn't have had to tell anyone that.

The Phillies would only win one more time before DiMaggio's hit streak ended on July 16.

At least Joe DiMaggio would get to play tomorrow.

When the heat of the summer bears down,
On all who must stay close to town.
A cool bath is nice,
Or a long drink with ice,
But careful; the Phillies might drown.

July 6–9

In two days' time, Cy Blanton would be in Detroit, pitching in the All-Star Game. Or at least, he'd have the chance to pitch in the All-Star Game. There were plenty of respected hurlers ahead of him on the depth chart. And none of them were getting shelled by the Giants on July 6.

The city of Chester had turned out to see Danny Murtaugh, their hometown boy, debut at Shibe Park. He and the more dangerous Danny, Danny Litwhiler, did a lot of the hitting that day, but Blanton got smashed back into the Phillies' clubhouse, where at least he was out of the rain.

In the ninth, with the Phillies down 7-3, Ike Pearson threw a single strike. A sopping wet umpire waved his hands and the game was over.

It was just as well. All the Phillies were going to do for a while was lose.

They had set up a pair of exhibition games to keep themselves in playing shape over the break, or whatever they thought playing shape was. Even their all-star, Cy Blanton, was rumored to be joining them as it did not conflict with his all-stardom. Doc Prothro said Blanton might even start one of the games before heading to Detroit.

Blanton's all-star selection made him only the fourth man on the Phillies roster to have been an all-star—Chuck Klein, Lee Grissom, and Merrill May being the others. Blanton had a 6-6 record, and though he had pitched four complete games including one seven-strikeout gem, his 3.92 ERA and the fact that he'd gotten his doors blown off by the Giants in his last start before the All-Star Game made it clear his selection was largely obligatory. Still, he was listed among the National League pitchers who had made his teammates look like fools at the plate, and Blanton had also benefited from not having to face one of the best players of all time who was in the middle of one of the best seasons of all time.

The NL, wrote Cy Peterman, was said to have "looked better than the gunners in the rival circuit, where Joe DiMaggio continues to rap everyone with an impartiality both magnificent and amazing."[1]

To take Peterman at his word, it would seem DiMaggio's streak had started to bore him as he took dead-eyed hacks that sent emotionless line drives up the middle. It didn't matter who was pitching; DiMaggio had entered a state of elite regularity that all he had to was swing and history seemed to make itself.

Up in Allentown, the Phillies were preparing to play their first exhibition against their own affiliate, the Allentown Fleetwings, a team the Phillies had borrowed for a year between its affiliations with the Cardinals. The day before, the grounds crew had burned gasoline on Allentown's Fairview Field to try to dry it out. But on July 8, the rain outmaneuvered them by continuing, so the mud was ankle-deep and the ball was covered in slop.

When the game started, the fire was out but there was still standing water in the infield. Because the gate had been so robust and the fans had filled the ballpark to the brim, the game was played despite the weather insisting it be called. Doc Prothro was glad to see some of the organization's prospects in person, but part of him had to view the game as a slump breaker of sorts. Nothing gets your mojo back faster than beating up on a bunch of your own prospects: Stan Benjamin hit two homers and the Phillies had 17 hits, bashing their farm team 11-3.

That was the kind of win the Phillies never pulled off against big-league teams. Maybe they should have just played exhibition games forever. They set up another one on July 9 against the U.S. Army's 44th Division squad and soundly defeated America's heroes at Fort Dix, too.

Ten thousand soldiers came out to watch the game and the Phillies didn't let their fellow countrymen make it much of one, trouncing the military men 15-0.

"It marked the first time a major league team has played in an Army camp since the selective service law went into effect," the Associated Press informed everyone.

The Phillies did their best to make sure it would never happen again. Maybe they thought if they beat the Army badly enough they'd end the draft. But a war needs bodies more than it needs a ball game.

Freed from the burden of the game mattering, Doc Prothro was feeling *good*. Something about pounding the life out of the U.S. Army and the score not being real really brought out the scamp in him. Or maybe he'd been hearing the Rogers Hornsby rumors, too, and figured, what the hell?

"Doc Prothro felt so good he took over third base himself," it was reported. "He fanned once, popped out, had an assist, and committed an error."[2]

Or maybe he'd just lost his mind.

But the stars of baseball weren't at Fort Dix that July, as Doc Prothro chugged an extra soda and cackled like a madman at third. They gathered in Detroit at Briggs Stadium for one of the greatest all-star games of all time.

Phillies manager Doc Prothro batting in an exhibition game against the 44th Infantry Division at Fort Dix on July 9, 1941. (Photo courtesy of Robert Warrington)

The American League was going for its sixth win in nine years. Bob Feller threw three shutout innings, striking out four for the American League. Arky Vaughn homered twice for the National League. Pete Reiser committed two errors. Both teams had a reliever blow a save. There were heroes and goats waiting for the game to end so that glory could be bathed in and shame could be assigned. It all depended on the outcome, which in the ninth inning had never been closer.

In a game rich with stars, it still all came down to DiMaggio. Vaughn's dingers had put the Senior Circuit up 5-3, but DiMaggio had delivered in the eighth. Twice.

His presence alone elicited a "shrill, spontaneous outburst" from the crowd, as though they hadn't been expecting him, though there's nothing spontaneous about a player being seen on the field after being heralded by the public address announcer. Nevertheless, the high-pitched sound being shrieked in unison at Joe DiMaggio proved well-earned. He doubled to deep left center and from second base watched Ted Williams blow a chance to knock him in by striking out, courtesy of Claude Passeau. With two gone, DiMaggio was in danger of being abandoned. Fortunately, DiMaggio stepped in.

Dom DiMaggio, younger brother of the base runner, stepped into the box. He was hitting .308 by that point in the summer, which was pretty good, as long as there was no reason for him to be compared to one of the greatest players of all time for the rest of his career and life. So Dom's pretty good numbers had no reason to be considered anything but that—pretty good. Unless you were, again, unfairly comparing them to a guy on a historic hit streak just because they shared the same blood and lack of interest in being fishermen.

The media didn't hang on Dom's every word like they did with his brother, but his last name was "DiMaggio," so they'd let him talk. He told some reporters that he'd taken up golf at one point but then given up after one try at it. Feeling chatty, the youngest DiMaggio would explain how it took him typically seven tries to get off the tee and, since he refused to retrieve his balls off the rough, he would run out of them four holes short of 18.[3]

But, if Dom was ever worried that his personal anecdotes weren't compelling enough, he was about to live one he could retell for generations. Preferably while Joe was standing next to him.

With his brother on second, Dom crushed a double to deep left center and Joe came Yankee Clipp-ing home. Now the National League's lead was down to one, and both DiMaggio boys were ready to play hero. Two of them were, anyway; Vince was off somewhere, thinking about how many hits he'd been robbed of in 1941 because Danny Litwhiler was playing too close to the line.[4]

The game was 5-4 now. Cy Blanton sat quietly on the National League bench, making zero impact. The NL offense went 1-2-3 in the ninth, sealing their fate. And never had fate been more apparent, or inevitable, than when DiMaggio came back to the plate.

It was Joe this time.

Claude Passeau had just walked a runner to load the bases with one out. Now he had to pitch to Joe DiMaggio. It might be the worst place in which a pitcher could find themselves in a game that doesn't count.

Once more, DiMaggio stepped out of the dugout; once more, the crowd made their sounds. They were about to see Joe DiMaggio win the All-Star Game. They'd get to tell that story forever. They were set at cocktail parties for life. Cy Blanton may or may not have been watching as closely as everyone else, or not at all. There is no record of his actions at this time.

But it's hard to be a hero when you hit a double play ball. The moment was either too big—or not big enough—for Joe DiMaggio as he knocked a grounder to short. Fate didn't like that at all, and suddenly the Dodgers' Billy Herman couldn't handle the relay, making DiMaggio safe at first. He may not have won the game, but he didn't end it. Fortunately, the American League had plenty of heroes left.

Ted Williams stepped out of the dugout.

Later, Cy Blanton packed his stuff in the National League locker room and headed home without making a single comment out loud, or at least one that was written down, about how he'd traveled to Detroit to sit on the bench for a night while Claude Passeau was left in to pitch three all-star innings all by himself. But Ted Williams was surrounded in the American League locker room by shouting reporters and gushing teammates. He'd hit the third pitch of his at-bat a "country mile," exclaimed the cartwheeling American League skipper, Del Baker, and won his team the game. Then Baker gave Williams a kiss on the cheek.

Williams had said he was swinging late all night but had known he would get in front of one before the end of the game. "I just wanted to beat the hell out of them," he said about the National League, back when players said things like that.[5]

Williams, 22 years old at the time, was plenty aware of DiMaggio's streak. He played in left field within earshot of the Fenway park scoreboard operator, who'd yell to him what DiMaggio had done after each at-bat. Ted would then pass the news on to Joe's brother Dom, who was playing next to Williams in center for the Red Sox.[6]

Williams' view of DiMaggio is distinct, as they both achieved a definitive statistical accomplishment in 1941 and therefore had a perspective of one another no one else on the planet could have had—two athletes at the top of their sport glancing curiously at one another across the standings. Williams was the only player considered comparable to DiMaggio as time went on; in 1946, there was a rumor that they'd be traded for each other, until Red Sox owner Tom Yawkey asked the Yankees to throw in the "little guy you've got in left field," Yogi Berra. The deal fell through.[7]

So it's far from staggering, then, that Williams concluded he was the better hitter— DiMaggio would hit .408 during his 56-game hit streak, Williams would remind everyone in his autobiography that he'd hit .412 himself during that same span. On Memorial Day that season, Williams had had six hits in a doubleheader and a batting average 100 points higher than DiMaggio's. Though he did concede that DiMaggio was the better overall player: "Even when Joe missed he looked good."[8]

For a few weeks it had looked like Williams and DiMaggio would be going for the hit streak record as a tandem in a pair of parallel historic runs that almost felt too narratively driven to be unscripted. On May 15, when DiMaggio began his hit streak, Williams started one too. It lasted 23 games and ended when he went hitless in both games of a doubleheader on June 8, but that didn't stop the papers from calling him "the mightiest hitter in baseball."

He was also looking to rebrand. Williams had been known for being a bit cocksure, ornery, and snappish toward the people and reporters of Boston. They hadn't liked it when he insinuated he'd rather be a fireman than a ballplayer, referring to his time hanging out in a local firehouse, where he felt he got along better with those whom society considered "little people" rather than the glamorous facades and drooling mobs of celebrity life.

But now, Williams—taking his share of the blame, but careful not to take all of it—was calling a truce with the public.

In August 1956, during a game against the Yankees in front of the largest crowd since World War II, Williams would drop a fly ball. Angry with himself (and his shortstop for not helping him), Williams' rage was further ignited by the boos raining down. Then, when he made a running catch to end the same inning, the fans switched to cheers … and Williams became even *angrier*, claiming in his autobiography that he'd been ready to stab somebody due to his hatred of front-runners.[9]

But the fans found a way to love a guy hitting .436, and Williams found his own way to love them back—wave at them on the field while quietly cursing them out under his breath.

"They said I was a heel and I'll admit I had a lousy attitude," Williams said. "But I don't think I deserved all they wrote about me even though I have to admit the start of it all probably was my fault."[10]

"The Kid has grown up," a reporter confirmed.

By the all-star break in 1941, Williams had only been hitting around .400 for about three and a half months. He was just a skinny punk who had never won a batting title and refused to wear ties on road trips.

"Splendid Splinter," they called him. "Willow Walloper." "Toothpick Ted." He had a big bat but seemed to disengage on defense, practicing his swing between pitches, and he ran like a scarecrow that just figured out it was alive—but even then, only when he felt like it. Pop-ups and groundouts were not always worth the effort.

This did not make Williams any friends in the won't-somebody-think-of-the-children crowd. What if a little leaguer saw his lack of exertion and decided to never apply themselves to anything again? What if Ted Williams had witnessed some poor excuse for a ballplayer when he was young, never been inspired to give the sport his all, and robbed future

A black-and-white, full-length photograph showing Ted Williams crossing the plate after hitting the walk-off home run of the 1941 MLB All Star Game at Briggs Stadium. (Photo courtesy of the SABR-Rucker Archive)

generations of baseball fans from watching his greatness? Who had been the example *he* followed?

He didn't know. The best Williams could do was tell you who his hero wasn't.

"I had a picture of Babe Ruth on my wall, but my mother always made more of that than I did. Somebody would ask her, 'Who was Ted's idol?' and she'd tell them, 'Babe Ruth,'" Williams wrote in his autobiography. "The fact was I didn't have an idol."

"I wasn't really concerned about Babe Ruth. It was 3,000 miles to New York and that seemed like three and a half months to me … I followed the big-league teams, but I wasn't all the time digging into the sports pages, memorizing the averages, or listening to games on the radio. I was out *doing* it. That's all I cared about."[11]

Williams wasn't the first ballplayer ever, but he almost seems like he was: the genesis of superstardom, the chicken before the egg, born exclusively from playing baseball, not watching it and impersonating a player's swing or attitude. Ted Williams was doing an impression of no one, and he would end the season by doing something no one had (or has) ever done. Williams may not have had an active hit streak, but he and DiMaggio were about to become idols to generations of baseball fans to follow, whether he'd quietly cursed them out or not.

The season's ceremonial midpoint had come and gone. Now, the second half would get underway, not just for the record-setters and chasers, but all players and teams, to tell the stories of how their seasons would end. Joe DiMaggio had hit safely in 47 straight games. Ted Williams had returned glory to the American League. The Phillies were a cool 30 games out of first place. Doc Prothro might have been mad with tooth rot.

Someone once wrote, "Managing the Phillies is like sticking your head in a bucket of water. If you stay at it long enough, you'll never be the same."[12]

Plenty of baseball left.

July 10–12

Half the summer gone.

A devastating moment for beachgoers, pool-sitters, day-trippers, and night-swimmers. Picnickers shiver at the fresh chill in the air; children fear the return of the school bus around the corner. Only several weeks remained for the joys of summer, and in 1941, the Phillies would do their best to ruin every one of them.

But Gerald Nugent's impatience may have been more than unconvincing theater. Word was he'd used the Phillies' exhibition game up in Allentown to scout the Fleetwings' young starter out of Millville, New Jersey, Andy Lapihuska, for the second time.

Both of Lapihuska's starts had been sterling, but they were just Interstate League starts; Lapihuska was still a couple of levels and a bunch of experience away from being major league ready, meaning he was beyond ready to play for the Phillies.

But! one newspaperman theorized, *what if Nugent's intention is to call up Lapihuska immediately? Certainly someone should write a column responding to that hypothetical situation!*

Millville seemed very protective of its ripe young arm. Even the nonzero chance that he'd be on the Phillies anytime soon was enough to rile them up. The local Millville paper wrote as though they feared Nugent was going to climb through an unlocked window and snatch Lapihuska away in the night.

They knew Lapihuska was talented. Their chief concern, which was the same concern of many in and outside of Millville, was that they also knew that the Phillies were the Phillies.

"After all, Philadelphia is a long way from being a topnotch ball club. Any pitcher making his major-league debut with the Quaker City unit is on the spot. He has anything but an airtight defense behind him, and his batting support is usually very ineffective."

Well that may be. But they were still—

"In such instances," the writer continued, "the opposing team usually runs up a one-sided victory margin, not so much through the inferior work of the pitcher as through the lack of support on the part of his teammates. It would not take very many bad beatings to completely upset the equilibrium of an aspiring young pitcher."

Sure, they get that. But the Phillies—

"Therefore," he went on, "although we may be wrong, it would be a much sounder idea for Lapihuska to have at least one season of advanced minor league experience under his belt before he attempts to take the bull by the horns. We do not for one minute doubt his ability to make the major league grade, but we do think that he will be better off in the long run if he makes the trek in easy stages rather than in one quick jump."[1]

It was settled. You hear that, Gerald Nugent? You won't be calling up Andy Lapihuska anytime soon, or you'll have the editorial board of *The Millville Daily* to contend with. So STAY ON YOUR SIDE OF THE RIVER.

No one wanted to watch their local phenom go to the majors if it meant going to the Phillies. Young pitchers who took the mound for them were never the same, like those managers with the water bucket. The Phillies would come out of the all-star break with a bang in 1941, but rather than an outburst of energy and motivation, the bang was more ominous, like an isolated gunshot in the distance.[2]

Take Tommy Hughes. The 21-year-old looked great for seven innings on July 10 as the Phillies built a 3-1 lead in their first game after the all-star break. Then he walked in two runs as part of a five-run Pirates rally and the Phillies lost, 6-3. Nick Etten kept doing the Lord's work from the batter's box, homering and singling in a run, but what was the point?

That Millville newspaper was right. The Phillies couldn't win. They could try to scout the sandlots for small fish to drop into their big, evaporating pond. But then they'd be out there gasping like everybody else.

They lost the next night, too, with Johnny Podgajny on the mound. Again, the eighth inning ate a young Phillies starter alive, as Podgajny let a 2-1 Pirates lead explode into a 6-1 Pirates win.

Now, the Yankees—there's a team on which a hometown boy could make good. Joe DiMaggio had hit safely in 51 straight games! The Yankees were battling for the top of the American League! You couldn't say a bad word about Joe anymore—or even a kind word about someone who *wasn't* Joe.

After getting a mailbox full of complaints on his Please-don't-forget-George Sisler piece, *Inquirer* columnist Cy Peterman was forced to respond the only way he knew how: sarcastically.

Peterman wrote that "corkscrew thinkers" had "whipped themselves into an unnecessary uproar."

"This is becoming a peculiar habit with sports fans," his piece read. "Write about Tom, Dick or Harry and they go into their dance of imaginary injury to Alf, Fred, or Otto."[3]

A wise insight from Peterman, who had, again, spent a lot of time defending Sisler's legacy from its zero attackers. The Sisler angle to all the DiMaggio stuff was picking up momentum, though, as writers began bringing up the old St. Louis Browns slugger as a fresh take on the DiMaggio narrative. Doc Prothro was asked how "Gorgeous George" compared to "Joltin' Joe" and Prothro pointed out that Sisler probably had two more hits a week than DiMaggio was currently getting because as a lefty, he started a step or two closer to first base.[4]

But in the end, Peterman had a tongue bath waiting for DiMaggio like everybody else, explaining that his Sisler column was out of simple appreciation at a point when the man might have been at his most forgotten.

"We like Joe," Peterman said, speaking seemingly for himself and the voice in his head. "We think he's among the great ball players of all time … His batting form is remarkable, he's a splendid sportsman, he's the key to the Yankee attack, an agreeable fellow on and off the field, and besides, he's kind to his mother. Is there anything further we need to say?"[5]

What was there *left* to say? The last DiMaggio-hater had been brought to heel and all there was to do was watch the star make more history.

Phillies outfielder "Dangerous" Dan Litwhiler. (Photo courtesy of the SABR-Rucker Archive)

DiMaggio was making trick shots now; he got his 49th hit in a game cut to five innings by rain, and his 50th hit was his 20th home run of the season. Whether baseball fans were staring expressionlessly at the Phillies or clapping like seals at Joe DiMaggio's latest well-struck ball, they would watch until it was over and then, in the Phillies' case, leave without buying a hot dog.

But in a gradually loudening Ringtown tavern in the Pennsylvania countryside, a few strangers started drinking and doing what strangers do when they drink, talking baseball. They talked a *lot* of baseball. But only about the Litwhiler boys, who'd come up on the ball fields of Ringtown.

The Phillies' Litwhiler, Danny, had taken his sweet time finding his swing in 1941, but he'd found it, and that was good enough. The chatty Kathies bought another round and toasted to Litwhiler's great arm and power bat, tracing his local history back through first-hand accounts and colloquial legends all the way to the major-league career the kid had now.

But Litwhiler had brothers—three or four of them, the group decided—and one of them, Woody, was an even *better* ballplayer. Maybe. Some agreed, some didn't, but it was generally conceded that Danny's older brother could really serve 'em over the pan.

But Woody was teaching school in Jersey now—never took the game too seriously, you see. Might have had a real shot at the bigs, that Woody. Scouts would come looking for arms in backwoods and jerk waters all the time. You never know who an arm like Woody's is going to bring to town.[6]

But that is the way of things in baseball. You can be buried in a small town box score and find your way to the Polo Grounds. You can hear God calling your name until you know how a baseball feels in your hand. You can have your bags packed for college but tell the driver to take you to the ballpark. You can bleed your heart out in a letter and hope it gets in the right hands; you can have a great day on the sandlot and hope you caught the right eye. And you can have a heater that really pops but still want to teach kids the fun of geometric proofs.

"It's the way things work out sometimes," the Ringtown crowd concluded.[7]

Baseball's history isn't full; it has endless space between the moments we know for the moments we don't.

Anywhere, anytime, somebody's stepping up to the plate. Maybe they take a couple pitches; maybe they're up there to hack. Maybe they make some solid contact; maybe they get caught looking. And they'll circle the bases or they'll walk back to the bench and they'll get a few quiet seconds to live in it before they're thinking about what happens next.

And whether they know it or not, they've changed, and how they've changed is going to change somebody else. Their next time up, that curve isn't as unhittable or they catch one in the spine. In a sport this old, not everything *can* matter. But when you step in that box, it's the only thing that does.

July 13–15

July 13 was Frank "Lefty" Hoerst Day at Shibe Park. Like any party for a 23-year-old man, the Phillies knew exactly who to invite: the assistant rector from the parish in which he was born.

Hoerst was the perfect player to honor before a game in Philadelphia, because he was *from* Philadelphia. He was no stranger to pitching in front of crowds, either. At 19 years old in 1937, he'd been pitching for the Burlington Cardinals. In one game, his teammate, George "Zum" Lapointe, was to be honored, and the 3,231 fans that came out to pack Centennial Field in Burlington, Vermont made up the biggest crowd of any Northern League game ever. Every seat had an ass, and for 10 minutes after the game had started, a steady stream of spectators continued to flow into the ballpark. Lapointe's popularity in his hometown of Winooski, Vermont, had brought everything there to a screeching halt.

"It was rumored a stranger tried to ask street directions in Winooski yesterday but couldn't find a single person," read one account. "At length, he discovered somebody listening to a radio, but 'Zum' Lapointe was at bat and he couldn't get a coherent answer. Yes, all of the mill town must have been at Centennial Field."[1]

Hoerst, unnerved by the amount of eyeballs looking down at him, did his best to steal the spotlight from Lapointe, the afternoon's top celebrity, with eight innings in which he "had the visitors eating out of his good left pitching hand."

Always an honorer, never the honoree. But the day was Hoerst's now, and he knew it was also a day on which any brash young challengers would get extra satisfaction by beating the man of honor. Something about tearing a man down in front of his loved ones really gets the competitive juices flowing.

It had been performances like his eight-inning highlight reel in Burlington that had gotten him the interest of a few big-league teams. Hoerst went to his old mentor and high school coach, Jocko Collins, for advice on which team he should sign with. Out of the New York Giants, Chicago White Sox, and the Phillies, Collins suspiciously pushed Hoerst toward the Phillies. And when they'd both gone to a meeting with Gerald Nugent, Nugent offered Hoerst *and* Collins contracts to be a pitcher and a scout for the Phillies, respectively.

Nugent may have been hitting the cherry brandy that afternoon, giving out jobs to whoever walked into his office.[2] Or perhaps the position was why Collins had nudged his client toward Philadelphia. Trickery and subterfuge are very effective ways to build a ball club.

Hoerst's had been a brief season in 1941, only starting in June. He'd been coaching basketball over the winter and broken his ankle, which, according to doctors, really hurt his ability to pitch. Now he was trying to make up for time he'd lost; and on July 13, baseball was in no hurry to have him back.[3]

Up until the 2020s, there was a time when any baseball game could go on forever. A lot of players hated it, a lot of writers hated it, the commissioner hated it; the only ones who liked it were the sickos watching from home using it as an excuse to open another beer.

Then commissioner Rob Manfred took his full mouth off of a billionaire's boot long enough to add clocks and ghost runners to baseball in an effort to make it shorter and more palatable to people who don't drink on Tuesday nights. Suddenly every game was wrapped up before the witching hour and America was going to bed on time. Thanks a *lot*, Rob.[4]

But back in 1941, you could still be playing ball when the sun came up—and there was no concern about the game changing in new, strange ways, unless maybe Joe DiMaggio was at the plate.

"I find this is the best spot to play DiMaggio!" exclaimed a player in a comic strip standing in the Yankee Stadium bleachers.

By now, DiMaggio had his eyes on another record: his own. In the minors, he'd hit safely in 61 straight games, a streak that had ended when all he could manage was a game-winning sac fly. On his worst night in two months, he had still won his team the game. He'd been a teenager then. Now, they called him "the Yankee Big Boy."[5]

Now that DiMaggio was at 55 straight big-league contests with a hit, everyone just assumed he was like a baseball game; theoretically, he could just keep going forever. But DiMaggio would've settled at 62.

On July 15, he singled and doubled and was intentionally walked. But they probably would have awarded him hit number 55 if he'd waved his cap at the crowd. He even hit a double play ball right at the White Sox in the first—but they didn't want it and gave him a free RBI instead by bungling the easy twin killing.

Even Ted Williams said DiMaggio was the best hitter in the league, and writers took the opportunity to compare their heights and weights and inches between their feet when they took their batting stance, just to get DiMaggio's name in the paper as many times as they could.

The previous Christmas, a column had been run "reporting" the innermost desires of various sports figures. National League president Ford Frick's wish was said to be "an NL team to beat the Yankees." It would have been nice for Frick to get the chance to stand tall above the AL, to speak with pride about NL players, to plan for celebrations of epic accomplishments, instead of just tipping his cap to the Yankees. The All-Star Game had been a brief salve the three times his league had won it, but the real trophy was still handed over in October.

Instead, on July 15, Frick was having an emergency league meeting with team owners in Detroit about how much the Phillies sucked.

"We know they have a problem and we are going to try and help them solve it," Frick said, likely shaking his head and staring hopelessly at the horizon.[6]

The Phillies being a problem was now a problem for more than the Phillies. They were leasing Shibe Park from their American League colleagues, the Athletics, and forking over 10 percent of the gate receipts to do so. The A's were guaranteed a minimum of $20,000 from this deal, which any *real* ball club would be able to cover over the course of a season.

"There has been no attendance to speak about," read the *Inquirer* on July 14. "And hence there's no surplus cash with which to build. The selling of players has run its course, destroying public loyalty over the years, and since too much of that increment was used for other purposes, the club is now stuck with minor leaguers."[7]

Yep. That ... pretty much summed it up.

But before they solved the problem of their ongoing last-place streak, their infectious unprofitability, and their failure to sell baseball's most easily sold concession item (that was actually three problems), on July 15, the Phillies had to first solve the problem of the Cardinals.

They would not solve that problem, nor any of the other ones.

It was the sixteenth inning of a 2-2 tie when the light bulb finally went on in the Cardinals dugout: We don't have to beat the Phillies, they realized. We just have to let them lose.

It was something they should have picked up on long before the game's unspeakable three-hour mark, given that their first run of the day was scored when Phillies second baseman Danny Murtaugh lost a ball in the sun.

They could have figured out that "losing" was the Phillies' default setting in the eleventh, too, when the Phillies loaded the bases with no outs and, with no idea what to do next, quickly racked up three outs and retreated to their dugout.[8]

Instead, St. Louis couldn't break the tie. The Phillies and Cardinals blasted right through the ninth into baseball's abyss. Ike Pearson was on his seventh inning of relief, equaling that of the Phillies' starter on the day. It was his longest non-starting appearance of the season, except for July 22, when he had to pitch 7.1 innings because Johnny Podgajny couldn't get out of the first. They'd lose that game by a run, too, but at least it had ended after regulation.

Nick Etten and Chuck Klein had managed a couple of scoreless singles in the thirteenth. That was the last time anybody had seen the Phillies' offense, which had proceeded to whiff their way through a couple of frames to reach the sixteenth, all while Pearson singlehandedly fended off Cardinal attacks, allowing only two hits. The reliever watched as the Phillies 1-2-3'd their way out of the fifteenth and grabbed his glove.

When a team sucks across the board, you're typically waiting to see which of their flaws will surface first and get the focus in the write-up. But as the Phillies tried to squeeze out a single run, knowing the moment they touched home plate the game would mercifully end, it became clear their offense wasn't going to win them this one. Pearson did his job, but they'd need to rely on him and the defense one more time to give their terrible offense another chance to not do what they'd been doing all day, which was again, nothing.

But the Phillies, of course, couldn't rely on anyone. Not their hitters, not their pitchers, not their team president. They couldn't even rely on their fans to buy hot dogs. And as the sixteenth frame came around, everything they hadn't been relying on still buckled under the weight of their incredibly low expectations.

Cardinals pinch hitter Johnny Hopp had been swapped into the game for Coaker Triplett in the eighth. Hopp was now coming to the plate for his fourth at-bat, meaning the game had gone long enough for him to have more plate appearances than the pitcher he'd replaced.

Hopp had weakly grounded out twice since singling off Boom-Boom Beck. He attempted to do so a third time by hitting a routine roller down to Etten at first base. But Hopp's speed kicked in as he raced down the baseline, and Etten couldn't get the ball to the bag in time to prevent a lead-off runner.

Johnny Mize came up next and thunked a bunt back to Pearson on the mound. With the runner in motion behind him, Pearson fielded the ball and fired a throw to first that was as ill-fated as it was off target. With runners now safely on first and second, Pearson finished the trifecta with a quick walk of Enos Slaughter, filling the bases with no outs.

By now, it was the longest game the Phillies had played in over 20 years. Reporters thumbed through the archives and found that they'd gone 21 innings against the Braves in 1918, in a game that they'd also lost, also by one run, giving them a glimpse into what the future held for them.[9]

It took almost no time for the next hitter, Jimmy Brown, to whack the game-winning fly ball to left field. Hopp raced home, the Cardinals took the lead, Pearson retired the next two hitters, and the Phillies' offense was ready to blow their last three chances. They slapped three grounders to the left side and everybody went home.

Coca-Cola ads all over the city told them what to do next: *"When the ball game's over … pause and turn to refreshment."* The smiling ballplayer featured in the ad made it clear this was not a man who'd just played in the Phillies' lengthiest loss of 1941. He was a happy man, a victorious man; a man rewarding his hard play and star-spangled spirit with a swig of ice-cold Coca-Cola.

"*You taste its quality!*" the ad assured everyone.

How Doc Prothro didn't have a promo deal with a soda company is simply a lapse in marketing from everyone involved. Perhaps he was disqualified from the ads due to the requirement of happiness, victory, and hard play.

But the people leaving Shibe Park had neither seen nor tasted quality on July 15, leaving the Phillies uncelebrated and their sodas unslurped. Stan Baumgartner called the 3-2 loss a "heartbreaker," another showcase of the team's inefficiencies that kept them forever in last place.

This one had just taken a little longer.

July 16–17

The day Doc Prothro had been born in 1893, the Phillies didn't lose. They won the day before and they lost the day after, but as James Thompson Prothro joined the world, the Philadelphia Phillies didn't have a game to play. They simply sat atop the standings, enjoying first place.

Neither a squealing baby Prothro nor a Phillies team that would eventually finish fourth were aware that they were on a fateful collision course. Almost 50 years and a single postseason appearance later, Prothro was wearing a Phillies uniform on his birthday, July 16—the day before Joe DiMaggio finally stopped hitting.

There was still plenty of history being made in baseball, however. On an almost daily basis, somewhere in the country, there would appear a bemused note in the local paper simply *marveling* at the 1941 Phillies' season, as though word of their squalidness was traveling from town to town like a campfire tale. Like they could sense the glory of DiMaggio's run was about to wrap up and they could all be morbidly entertained by this Phillies team that had apparently been losing the whole summer.

"According to the books, the Philadelphia National League team was at its worst in 1883, when the Phillies won only 17 games all season," wrote one columnist. "The clubs played only 77 games and called it a year in those days, however, and if the 1941 outfit continues its current pace, a new modern mark will be established."

"Even for a Philadelphia club," he added, unnecessarily.[1]

Given their reputation, what came next was surprising for the Phillies. Ford Frick had spent the 1941 season doing two things: having meetings about how the Phillies were ruining everything, and denying requests to bring the spitball back. So it was startling when he offered the Phillies the chance to host the 1943 All-Star Game at Shibe Park.

They'd already had the All-Star Game in New York. Chicago. Boston. D.C. Detroit. Cleveland. New York a second time. Cincinnati. St. Louis. And though the 1942 All-Star Game didn't have a location yet, there were some rumors circulating. Possibly New York?

There was only one more two-team city that hadn't hosted the event, and since the Phillies hadn't been downgraded from a ball club to an incompetent street gang yet, Philadelphia still qualified. It would be the 60th anniversary of their existence (something some owners felt the league was still being punished for) and the 10th anniversary of the All-Star Game itself. What better place to put it than Philadelphia?

But Nugent said no. He may have been strapped for cash, but he wasn't strapped for honor.

In an act of gentlemanly class, or perhaps of not wanting to do the work, Nugent told Frick that the Phillies leased Shibe Park from the Philadelphia Athletics, so Connie Mack and *his* team should be considered the hosts instead. Philadelphia would still get the game, he explained, but the Mackmen would be at the forefront, not the Phillies, who would likely be in last place by then.

Frick had originally asked Nugent if the Phillies would like the 1942 All-Star Game. But the host of the Midsummer Classic traditionally shifted from American to National League parks every year, and with at least five years before a city could get it again after hosting, Nugent didn't want Mack and his AL team unable to host for the next few years if the Phillies hosted in 1942. So by pushing Philadelphia's hosting duties to 1943, the city still got the game and the A's got to host. It was win-win. Except for Nugent.

Frick might have left that meeting shaking his head. Why couldn't he be dealing with stoic, impressive, crowd-drawing *American* League baseball, where Joe DiMaggio was reminding everyone what it was like to be an *American* and distracting everyone from global horrors with the novelty of sport? Instead, he was talking to Gerald Nugent, who again seemed to have really gone out of his way to avoid any kind of personal victory.[2]

But at 56 straight games with a hit, even DiMaggio was in danger not just of losing his streak every night, but of another, more horrifying prospect: boredom.

The same thing too many times, even a good thing, leads a national audience to yawn and stretch and see what else is on.

As the author of a letter to the *Philadelphia Inquirer*, identified only as "Andy," put it, DiMaggio was nearing the point at which his success was so reliable it had become too predictable.

"The daily monotony of Joe DiMaggio's hitting calls to mind the advice of an old city editor," Andy wrote. "'If a man jumps out of a 10-story hotel window and is killed, it's news. If he jumps out and lives it's a sensation. If he jumps out the second time and lands unhurt it's an established scientific miracle. But if he does it a third time, it's just a publicity stunt.'"[3]

We will never know who Andy was, where he would have heard an editor say such a bulky, unwieldy quote, or how genuinely he was comparing DiMaggio's hit streak to a man trying repeatedly to kill himself.

But we do know that it meant not everybody was applauding DiMaggio's crusade anymore. The thrill, for some, was gone. The man grabs his bat, he goes to the plate, he collects his hit, and we all wait until tomorrow. After two months, history was getting a little old.

At this point, it was news when DiMaggio did *not* hit, with the flabbergasted AP reporting he had grounded out once against Cleveland (between singling in the first and doubling in the ninth). DiMaggio hitting his way on base was as normal to America as not being involved in World War II yet. And for his 56th trick, DiMaggio and the Yankees crushed Cleveland for their 16th win in 17 games with a yawn.

But in the home of the 1943 All-Star Game, things remained quite shameful. The *Inquirer*'s "Imagine My Embarrassment" column, which published tales of local humiliation sent in by readers, ran a pair of stories: one about a person leaving an item behind at the grocery store, and one about a woman who had some bobby pins fall out of her hair.[4] A whole city of red-faced fools, yet the section featured nothing about the baseball team down the street that had already lost 60 games and buried itself 34 games out of first place.

The Phillies were set to play two against the Cubs in Philadelphia on July 16 with Tommy Hughes back on the mound. The young stud seemed to be pitching every day, but given how often the Phillies lost, that wasn't good news. Even taking on the Cubs, who'd only won two of their last 10, would be a challenge.

The Phillies did not have to imagine their embarrassment as it became quite real in the first inning. Hughes gave up three runs pretty quickly, one of which came on a home run from the Cubs pitcher. The next two innings, the Phillies tied it up at 3-3, and when they seemed suspiciously close to a two-out rally, Prothro found a pinch hitter for Hughes and the young hurler's day was done.

The tie lasted only a few minutes as Cubs catcher Clyde McCullough bashed a three-run homer in the third, and some more runs trickled in as each member of the Phillies bullpen came in to try to give it a go. The Phillies lost, 9-5, as elsewhere, Joe DiMaggio stroked the final hits of his historic streak.[5]

A clutch of summer showers were baptizing the North Atlantic into the season's dog days. The Phillies' July 16 game against the Cubs had been a bit soggy, and the moisture was said to continue into the next day's contest. Hughes, picking the mud out of his spikes, was likely glad to get in and out of his start without a humiliating pratfall (though getting pulled without recording an out probably stung a bit).

The next day, as DiMaggio geared up for number 57, it was Johnny Podgajny's turn.

Podgajny's horoscope (he was a Gemini, *of course*) informed him the morning of July 17 that there were "very good indications … for your particular line of endeavor, and ROMANCE."[6]

Would the young man find love … *and* his fastball? The stakes had never been less meaningful on the standings!

Podgajny and his Cubs counterpart, Vance Page, both allowed multiple base runners in the first but kept the scoring off the board. Neither of them allowed a run for the first three innings, though their complete lack of a 1-2-3 frame between the two of them indicated that the runs were there, just waiting for the first hittable fastball over the plate to be scored.

The Cubs got it in the top of the fourth. With two outs and their catcher on second, Chicago sent Page, their pitcher, to the plate with a chance for an RBI. Page rolled a slow grounder to Phillies shortstop Bobby Bragan. Writers weren't entirely sure whom to blame for what followed—Bragan's low throw allowed Page to reach first safely, but Nick Etten's slow grab of it prevented him from throwing out McCullough plodding around third to score.

Nevertheless, it was 1-0 now. The game was a run or two from being dangerously out of reach. Fortunately, Phillies catcher Bennie Warren stole focus with a two-run blast to left off Page in the bottom of the inning, with Bragan having reached on a bunt in front of him, making it 2-1. The Cubs' Bill Nicholson wrecked Podgajny's offering in the fifth through the light standards of Shibe Park, dropping a little souvenir on the fans and streetwalkers meandering down 30th Street, and the game was tied 2-2.

The pitching duel caught many in the audience by surprise. Podgajny was 21 and hopes were still high, or at least medium, that he'd be a part of the team's more effective pitching staff in the future. But at the moment, his ERA was lingering just below 5.00. Page, on the other hand, had never made a big-league start before, and had been so unfamiliar with the custom that he told the Cubs manager he wasn't even sure how long to warm up.[7]

And then, nature stepped in.

With the game tied at 2-2 in the sixth, a pair of Cubs took their hacks before the skies opened and the rain came down in sheets. The players were called off the field and everyone decided that enough was enough—there was no reason to watch the Cubs and Phillies play three more innings even *before* the weather had interfered, but nobody was interested in doing so while dripping wet. The hundreds of women in attendance who'd had to flee from a completely exposed grandstand when the deluge had started likely agreed.

The Phillies may have failed to field cleanly, hit timely, win, or even finish a ball game, but the biggest failure of the baseball day on July 17 belonged to Joe DiMaggio.

Municipal Stadium in Cleveland was packed to the gills. Some were there to see DiMaggio keep the streak going. Some were there to celebrate its possible end. No matter their motivations for attending, the supporters, well-wishers, critics, and yawners made up the largest night-game crowd in baseball history to that point.

Much had been made of who the pitcher would be who would "end" DiMaggio's streak, as though one man and one arm would truly be the thing that broke 56 straight games of offensive production. It was skill, talent, and instinct that DiMaggio brought with him to the plate each time, but it was baseball he was playing, so luck was a factor in every moment as well. DiMaggio learned this the night his hit streak died.

Cleveland put two hurlers out there for DiMaggio to face, neither of whose accomplishments on the evening earned them a flattering description in the papers: There was "Portly Al Smith," whose screwball was known for its ignorance of physics, and there was "Jim Bagby, Jr.," identified as "the son of Old Sarge, who pitched Cleveland to a pennant in 1920." Just a pair of nobodies, it seemed, one with a family member whom you may recognize, and one who was fat; a quality so crucial in the telling that it was the first thing a writer wanted to tell you about him.

But it wasn't Smith or Bagby, Jr. who truly stopped the DiMaggio menace. Because he wasn't hitting balls at the *Phillies* defense, DiMaggio couldn't catch a break for the first time in two months, since he was hitting them at Cleveland's third baseman, Ken Keltner.

The 24-year-old Keltner was about 10 days removed from being a two-time all-star. Hitting .283 on the season by July 17, Keltner was also considered a defensive firecracker. He'd caught a bit of the press's wrath in 1939 when he'd asked for $15 a week in unemployment benefits during the winter months. Reporters had turned to him, prepared to scoff and laugh, until Keltner had told them it was a joke, which for some reason had pissed them off even more.[8]

But Keltner made the Clevelanders happy on July 17. DiMaggio came up to bat in the first, did nothing with Smith's first offering, and then slashed a grounder down the third base line. Keltner got a bead on it, lurching to his left and making a backhanded stab before the ball could get by him. Then came the tough part: getting it across the diamond. DiMaggio, of course, was also pretty quick, but Keltner reared back and fired to first base with enough juice on his throw to nail the Yankee Big Boy by half a step.

DiMaggio walked in his next at-bat, which, given how his night ended, offered a solid one-time counterargument to modern baseball's adage, "a walk's as good as a hit." In the seventh, he returned to the plate having gone nowhere but 0-for-1. And again, he tried to clip one past Keltner at third. But Keltner was locked in. Once more, he made a backhanded stop across his body, sent the ball to first as quickly as he could, and caught DiMaggio with some air between his cleat and the bag.

DiMaggio did get another chance in the eighth, and wisely kept the ball away from Keltner. Unfortunately, every other infielder got a turn to touch it, as DiMaggio grounded into a 6-4-3 double play. The Yankees managed to win, 4-3, finding heroes in Lefty Gomez and Red Rolfe, but not Joe DiMaggio, who departed from the stadium in a state of utter hitlessness for the first time in months.

And the nation wondered …

Is it over?

What happens next?

Do we have to go to World War II now?

The next day DiMaggio went 2-for-4 with a double. He'd hit safely in his next 16 games. But by the end of August, he was just another greedy hold-out.

"Joe DiMaggio is a great ballplayer," read one newspaper that month. "But off the field, his only approach to color is his idea of what he is worth next year."[9]

The Rest of the Season

With no Joe DiMaggio to gawk at, the nation's gape-mouthed rubberneckers turned their attention to the trainwreck that was the Phillies, noticing their uncomplex pattern of play: a win or two every couple of weeks, surrounded on either side by about eight to 10 losses in a row.

"This sort of thing has been going on all season," one paper noted, as though stunned. "There seems to be nothing that can be done about it."[1]

The Phillies didn't lose *badly*, wrote one charitable sports-follower, but they certainly did lose *often*. And that was enough to leave them buried in the standings and forgotten by the crowds. If they wanted to avoid sinking down, down, down, to the depth of the historical record, they'd have to find the answers that had eluded them all season. And for a long time before that, as well.

So at some point in August, Doc Prothro left.

"Manager Doc Prothro recently decided his last-place Phillies couldn't be any worse without him and left the club to its own devices while he shook the bushes for help," read one account.[2]

A stated but unconfirmed sentiment from the Phillies' manager was that didn't see too many good players anymore, having watched the Phillies too closely. It was as good a time as any to go look at something else.[3]

Prothro seemed to have packed up a stick and bindle with his remaining sodas and slipped out a window into the night. He was needed elsewhere, or simply wanted to *be* elsewhere, and had abruptly decided, or had it decided for him, that the open road was calling.

The official word was that Prothro was scouting the International League for talent that could make the Phillies look like a baseball team. The whispered word was that Prothro was on his way out. His own competence was never challenged, only his ability to take a ragtag group of losers and turn them into winners. Sometimes, that leads to a group of underdogs winning at life through the power of friendship. But other times, putting a bunch of losers together simply leads to more losing, only as a group now.

Then, the rumor changed: Prothro *wasn't* on his way out; he was on his way *up*. The good dentist, it was believed, would be bumped up to general manager of the Phillies and Hans Lobert would take over as the skipper.

Lobert's biggest strength as a manager of this particular team was that he was already dead inside.

"Lobert has served as coach of the Phillies for eight years," it was written. "He is used to them."[4]

Finally, somebody asked Gerald Nugent just what the hell was going on, and Nugent calmly explained that it was all lies.

"There is no truth to the reports," he informed parties curious about Prothro's disappearance and his future role with the team. The Phillies' manager would, Nugent said, be back later in the week to finish out the homestretch with his terrible baseball team.[5]

But would he? One southern newspaper was proclaiming that their beloved Doc Prothro was returning to Tennessee to manage the Memphis Chicks of the Southern League in 1942, and they were not restrained in their contradiction of Nugent's words: "DOC'S COMING BACK," read the headline. "Doc Prothro figures life's too short to waste any more of his on such a hopeless proposition."[6]

The "hopeless proposition" was the Phillies, if that's not clear.

How does a team pass the time while their manager is on a break—not for health issues, not for a family emergency, but just to get away from them?

Well, the Phillies set a record for the number of baseballs used in a single game, though it must be said that the Cardinals *did* help. St. Louis outfielder Dan Padgett actually did most of the work, fouling 15 of them into the stands himself. So really, the Phillies didn't even contribute much to that milestone.[7]

The Phillies did manage to win two in a row once in early September. That was fun. They heard from Prothro, too, when he radioed back that the minor leagues offered plenty of talent to be acquired. Assuming the Phillies could acquire it, there *could* be a path forward toward more successful seasons in the years ahead.

"Sure, we're last," Gerald Nugent told reporters. "And a bad last, and this has been a disappointing season. But that doesn't mean my club is a complete bust."

Closing his office door before the deafening, collective response of "*Does it, though?*" was fired back at him, Nugent appeared to be very tired of reality; a reality the media was more than happy to lay out.

One writer cleared things up: "Faced by the chance of setting a new modern record for futility, the local club seems to face an immediate future as dismal as its recent past and its present, spiced by shutouts in double-headers, general all-around weakness and errors that reached a high of eight in one recent game."[8]

Nick Etten's slugging prowess was a topic sought out by reporters who'd noticed somebody on the Phillies was hitting .331 in August. Etten, who'd willed himself onto the roster with a strongly worded letter, was now said to hold the secrets of hitting the ball hard and far.

"Forget about being smart, says young Mr. Etten," read the story, "whose batting average of .331 indicates it's a pretty good plan."

That's right, kids—throw those learning books out the window and start taking hacks at anything that comes at you. Baseballs. Baseball-sized rocks. Beer cans. Butterflies. Etten explained it as though the second you start thinking fastball, you get a curve; the moment you settle in for a curveball, you get the heat. Might as well dump the whole "strategizing" component of your approach and remember you've got a wooden club in your hands.

"Just go up there and swing," Etten said. "Don't think."[9]

That mindset continued serving Etten well. In a game against the Cardinals, he doubled his way on base and watched Danny Litwhiler's 13th homer of the season sail out of the stadium to give the Phillies a 2-0 lead. The day then naturally devolved into a bone-cracking, mind-blowing loss as Bobby Bragan stepped on the hand of Cardinals shortstop Johnny Hopp, breaking it, and the Phillies suffered a walk-off loss in extras on an inside-the-park home run.[10]

Seemingly out of players to honor individually, the Phillies went about honoring local towns at Shibe Park. September 21 was deemed "Chester Day" and the two Phillies from Chester, Pennsylvania, Johnny Podgajny and second baseman Danny Murtaugh, were going to be honored; in Podgajny's case, again. Hopefully it would go better than his last honoring.

Murtaugh, not really one of the Phillies' main characters over the summer, had gotten a late start joining the team in June. But that meant he still had something of a grace period with the press, who would view his slowly rising batting average and repeated on-base episodes as a promise of potential, rather than a guarantee of disappointment. For now.

"Had he started with the club in spring training, Danny might have been around the .300 mark all year," one paper boldly assumed. "As it happened, the pitchers had a big edge on him when he came up."[11]

Boom-Boom Beck recorded his first win of the season on August 10. Frank Hoerst became the only pitcher in the National League without a win. Ike Pearson killed a rally against the Pirates by hitting a base runner with a grounder. Tommy Hughes' sister died.[12]

The first National Leaguer of 1941 to crush a home run in every ballpark,[13] Danny Litwhiler was hitting everything, including the trade block, as his batting average ballooned to .300 and the Giants and White Sox were willing to spend a tantalizing $6,500 to secure him—a number far too high for Gerald Nugent to ignore.

"After all, what can the Phillies offer a young slugger in the way of a future?" reasoned one writer.[14]

At the other end of baseball, for Joe DiMaggio, the rest of the season was a victory lap. When you hit safely in 56 straight games, resetting one of baseball's most fundamental records, you don't have to do too much more to be named MVP.

DiMaggio got a party. DiMaggio got a trophy. DiMaggio got a trip to the injured list for a little while after he sprained his ankle. The Yankees led Limpin' Joe into a hotel room and surprised him with a little shindig, then handed him a silver humidor with an image of himself swinging on it.

"Presented to Joe DiMaggio by his fellow players on the New York Yankees," read the inscription, "to express their admiration for his consecutive hitting record. 1941."[15]

If the Phillies had been led to a hotel room for a surprise, it would have been to be smothered with a pillow. Fortunately for them, all they received was a poem in their hometown paper about a familiar subject: how much they sucked.

> Dodgers and Phillies went out to play
> On a recent afternoon.
> And the Dodgers played so sweetly.
> The Phillies forgot the tune.[16]

As fate would have it, the Phillies and Dodgers would close out the 1941 regular season together, both happy for their respective endings.

The Dodgers were National League champions. They had climbed over the Cardinals and snatched the pennant right out of their hands, proving that even a team synonymous with the word "Bums" can, given enough years, find a way to the top.

It was an example that was good for the Phillies to see. In less than 10 years, they, too, would face the Yankees in the World Series. They too would see Joe DiMaggio in the flesh on baseball's biggest stage. And they, too, would lose.

But all of that would come later. On the final day of the 1941 regular season, the Phillies and Dodgers threw a party in Flatbush.

With actress Betty Grable seated in Dodgers manager Leo Durocher's private box, the Dodgers slapped the Phillies around for a few innings, letting a rookie named Bob Chipman pitch the first five innings of what would be a 12-year career. Another rookie, Pete Reiser, became the official NL batting champion. Durocher emptied his bench early, handing out playing time like confetti at a parade, and even jumped in to play shortstop for a little bit.

"Even the Phillies seemed to get into the spirit of the occasion," read the local paper.[17]

Maybe the Phils deserved a bit of fun, even if it was kind of at their expense. It had been a slog of a final two months. They were getting outdrawn by the Athletics at Shibe Park 3 to 1 and were obviously losing money. They'd gotten as hot as they'd ever be in August and won double-digit games in a month for the first and only time all season, going 11-20. Then they lost 22 of their last 29 games in September. Their final game of the regular season was the Dodgers' 100th win and the Phillies' 111th loss.[18]

And as they wrapped up their 1941 gauntlet in Brooklyn with poor play and weary smiles, reporters threw in one last little barb:

"Last Armistice Day … Larry MacPhail pulled a fast one. He bought Kirby Higbe. That transaction, which caught certain bidders flatfooted, may have clinched the 1941 pennant for Brooklyn."[19]

Down in the Phillies' hometown, the A's were finishing their season, too, facing Ted Williams and the Red Sox for their final nine frames. The award season chatter would be all about who the AL MVP was, DiMaggio or Williams, Williams or DiMaggio, and Williams had one more day of hitting over .400 in him.

"Now it was the last day of the 1941 season, and it turned up cold and miserable in Philadelphia," Williams wrote in his memoirs. "They still had 10,000 people in Shibe Park, I suppose a lot of them were just curious to see if The Kid really could hit .400. I have to say I felt good despite the cold. And I know just about everybody in the park was for me."

"As I came to bat for the first time that day, the Philadelphia catcher, Frankie Hayes, said, 'Ted, Mr. Mack told us if we let up on you he'll run us out of baseball. I wish you all the luck in the world, but we're not giving you a damn thing.'"[20]

Williams had gotten a gift in 1941: no hate mail. He was getting more letters than ever before, he said, but most of them were generously telling him to ignore his haters and not insulting him or drawing diagrams illustrating how to hit (anymore).

But there are no gifts in Philadelphia sports. You pay for everything. A two-out walk *will* come in to score. A struggling player *will* succeed elsewhere. A traded prospect will *certainly* be an MVP someday. Good fortune must be counterbalanced by bad luck; bad luck must always lead to mistakes; mistakes will always be paid for with failure.

Baseball will always come back, until the sun swallows the earth. And each spring, things are a little different, even if they end the same. The Phillies were still years away from contention in 1941, or even being very

Philadelphia Phillie signing autographs for four female fans at Braves Field. (Courtesy of the Boston Public Library, Leslie Jones Collection)

interesting, but after the Yankees celebrated their World Series, after the winter had covered the dirt with snow, after the warmth of springtime returned to the Delaware Valley, the players retook the field, the fans found their seats, and in that first beautiful moment, there was, as there always is, enough hope to last you until the fall.

Except for Doc Prothro. He was, in fact, fired, and he did, in fact, manage the Memphis Chicks. But like DiMaggio and Williams, Doc made his own history in 1941, too, finishing his big-league managing career with the worst winning percentage of all time (.301). He'd only managed the Phillies a short while—three seasons—but fortunately, his memory was even shorter.

Come spring in 1942, he looked out at his Chicks bumbling about the diamond, cursing at missed grounders, firing wild pitches 10 feet over the plate. Doc mopped his brow and shook his head.

"I've never had so many problems since I started managing a baseball club," he said.[21]

As a team that lost 111 games that everyone was eager to forget, the 1941 Phillies would go on to be referenced over the decades any time some Phillies squad did something truly awful. When a particular rough patch for the Phillies gets too long, you can know that you'll be hearing Doc Prothro's boys mentioned on the broadcast soon enough.

In 2014, another lousy Phillies team had lost well over 10,000 games (in franchise history, that is), and of their 84 most recent ones, 11 had been shutouts. Only one team in history, the media noted, had been shut out more times than that in their first 84 games of the season.[22]

Boom-Boom, Dangerous Dan, Johnny Rizzo, big Nick Etten, the bespectacled Johnny Podgajny, and all the rest of the ghosts from 1941 all nodded sagely from the clouds above, nestled safely in baseball heaven, where no fastballs down the pike are missed, no one ever falls off the mound, there are barely any stranglings, and the concession stands are always open, selling wiener after wiener.

Epilogue

Vince DiMaggio was hungry.

The Phillies and Pirates were supposed to play a night game in the summer of 1944 at Shibe Park, but it was called off and the 32-year-old outfielder needed something to eat. Sure, he could grab a meal at the Pirates' hotel like the rest of the team. But Vince was hungry for *change*, too. So he went out into the Philadelphia night and found a place with a floor show and a steak dinner.

"Vince doesn't remember if the steak was good or only excellent," it was reported later.[1]

Regardless of how they cooked it, it was a steak Vince would remember for a long time. He charged his six-dollar check to the Pittsburgh Pirates and headed back to the hotel, where he laid down his tired head and full belly and dreamt of one day hitting over .250.

The next time he got a paycheck, Vince noticed it was a little lighter. Ten dollars and 36 cents lighter, in fact. The Pirates had gotten wind of his off-the-books banquet and were sick of covering his extra expenses, as he'd also charged them for a four-dollar breakfast the morning before he'd snuck out for a steak. Vince claimed he'd only eaten one out of the five team meals he could have had while the Pirates had been in Chicago a few weeks prior, and said that by doing so he'd actually *saved* the team money—technically, *they* owed *him*.

The Pirates didn't want to hear that, and the dispute spilled into dramatic pronouncements of self-worth.

"If that's the way it is, okay," Vince told reporters. "If I'm not worth $6.36, then you can take this ball club and keep it."

The Pirates did keep their club. It was Vince they let go. Trade rumors started immediately after the argument, and Vince spent the next few days assuming he was headed to the New York Giants. His brother Joe sent him a letter from New York, a city they might be sharing soon, assuring Vince that he'd heard the deal was all but done.

A deal *was* done, but not the one Vince had wanted. Instead of New York, the Pirates dealt him to Philadelphia, a different city with a much worse baseball team. Vince claimed he was happy to go there, too, because he had always hit well in Shibe Park.[2]

Philadelphia may not, at one point, have been able to sell a lot of hot dogs. But it could sell you a real fateful steak.

And so, the closest thing to Joe DiMaggio ever putting on a Phillies uniform happened in the spring of 1945 when his brother Vince put one on. Vince would hit four grand slams in one season for the Phillies, setting a single-season franchise record while also leading the league in strikeouts. He was also punched in the face by a teammate for singing on a train.[3]

In short, he had a typical Philadelphia baseball experience.

At the end of the 1941 season, Joe DiMaggio collected his MVP award, threw in another all-star season for good measure, and then went to war for three years. This time, it was against the Nazis and not American League pitching (not that DiMaggio ever *saw* a Nazi, being stationed in New Jersey, California, and Hawaii). He returned stateside, continued being one of the greatest players of all time, and won another MVP award in 1947. He played his final big-league baseball game over 70 years ago.

Baseball fans latch onto their warmest memories from when they were children un-crushed by adulthood and believe that things were objectively better then, because it's the last time they can remember being happy and unburdened. We're all at the mercy of owners who view baseball as a revenue stream and a commissioner installed to keep them happy. You're lucky simply to have ever seen a version of baseball you actually loved.

DiMaggio is locked into eternity. His legacy and the era in which he built it is long over. But there's a lot that gets skipped, ignored, forgotten, or shrugged off. The Phillies, for much of their time in existence, haven't been beyond baseball, but seemed to be playing *next* to it; outliers playing a sillier version of the same game off to the side somewhere.

Before the 1941 season got underway, Gerald Nugent got an offer from a persistent young man named John B. "Jack" Kelly who headed a five-man syndicate that wanted to buy the Phillies for half a million dollars. Nugent waved them off.

But Kelly didn't like that answer, so he went to the National League president, Ford Frick. Frick had already spent part of the summer hearing about how the Phillies' shittiness under Nugent was hurting the rest of the league. Other owners didn't feel it was worth it anymore to send their clubs to Shibe Park, where the gate takes were low and the concession stands were shuttered. One owner even claimed his team couldn't afford to buy his players dinner in Philadelphia because ticket sales for their game had been so small. Presumably this was not the Pirates.

Nugent claimed he wasn't against spending his money. That had been his predecessor, William Baker, a famously stingy owner whose secretary Nugent had romanced and wed before being hired by the organization. But Nugent claimed he wanted to win. And he was just as good at wanting to win as the Phillies were at winning.[4]

Nugent needed an advance loan from the league office to even get the Phillies to spring training in 1942, and they had to temporarily change their name to the "Phils" due to complaints from the company that made Phillies Cigars.

As other teams ebbed and flowed through their various eras, the Phillies were nearby, trying to stand up on roller skates; the only team whose own diehards wouldn't pick them to win it all and the first team to lose more than anybody ever had. But they have a history, same as Joe DiMaggio.

We've learned in Philadelphia, in our time watching the Phillies (whatever that time was or is), that nothing is immortal or eternal. People have now seen multiple Phillies teams win the World Series in a single lifetime. They have seen the team spend beyond previously set limits. They have watched their reputation go from mediocre runners-up to the best rotation in baseball to failed rebuilders to unlikely pennant winners.

I wrote about these games from 1941 with a cocky certainty and snide little comments because they've already happened. It's the luxury of looking back on history, which has happened, instead of the challenge of forecasting the future, which has not.

But in every game they played, the 1941 Phillies took the field thinking they might not lose; or at least, preferring not to. They came to the plate thinking they could get a hit. They took the mound thinking they wouldn't get their cleat stuck in the mud and fall down. Maybe they didn't always *believe* they could win or *assume* they could win, but statistically, it was always possible. You come to the ballpark to play a ball game, and a ball game's only got two ways it can end.

String enough wins or losses together and they call it your history. Is it worth remembering? Yes. Because you can get a little bored reading about Joe DiMaggio. He made history, but he was only a part of it. And history is always happening, whether you're in the middle of it or not.

"It gives you something to think about when you're waiting for the fish to bite," Ted Williams wrote.[5]

Before the 1941 season had started, the Phillies had received an offer from a "mysterious syndicate" ready to pay $50,000 for the team, $250,000 for new players, and $250,000 for the farm system.

Reporters asked Gerald Nugent about it. He said he hadn't heard anything so they went to his legal adviser, Bob Irwin. Nobody had brought him an offer, Irwin said, but someone had asked about the possibility of doing so. When Irwin had asked whom they had represented, they'd refused to say.

Whoever's shadow agents they'd been, they hadn't stuck around long. And in any case, Nugent wanted it clear that, for the first time ever, he wasn't interested in making a buck.

"The Phillies," he said, "are not for sale."[6]

They lost 111 games.

It's easy to wonder how a team that was poorly funded, frequently inferior, incapable of executing, and easily defeated would survive years of waning interest in baseball, world wars, and loss after loss. But the Phillies were able to maintain their local support for a lot of reasons, but one of them was the sense of ownership felt not by Gerald Nugent or any of his successors, but by the fans and the city itself.

On the rare occasions when the Phillies have put a winner on the field, the fans can be challenging to entice. Their trust in a sports team, knowing fully how it feels to have that trust betrayed, is slowly, but inevitably rebuilt. But then, once everybody buys in, the Phillies are the biggest draw in town.

Of course, there are plenty of seasons in which they are jeered or ignored. In those cases, public support is sustained not through trust, but delusion.

No one is required to stay a fan when a team is being dumb, or cheap, or directionless. But being a fan means looking at the mess in front of you and shrugging and saying, "Well, those are our guys."

While the Athletics were still in town, Philadelphia took advantage of its two-team status by having them play each other for the city's amusement. The City Series was paused in 1941, due to dwindling attendance. The Phillies apparently couldn't even do numbers in their own city, in a game played exclusively for their fans.

The A's had a more prestigious history, but they were down there in the slop with the Phillies by August 1941. Still, they were 20 games better than the Phillies, who really "got" how to be a last-place team. They didn't flirt with outside chances or give fans a reason to hope; they just lost and lost and lost. The A's still had their dignity, at least—but the Phillies had Phillies fans. They weren't coming out to a lot of games, but they were waiting for a reason to, and they felt they now had a few.

"What's wrong with the Phillies?" asked one *Inquirer* writer. "Ask Phillies' fans—and your ear-drums very likely will be broken by the thunder of their reply."

Several of them were asked about the possibility of a *postseason* City Series, with the Phillies and A's facing off in a real playoff game, and all of the respondents spoke with the confidence of people who had been watching a different team all year.

"The A's have been drawing big crowds and still losing games. And the Phillies are a better team than the A's."

"Man for man, hitter for hitter, can any sports writer show me where the A's have a better team?"

"It is just that the fans are prejudiced and taught by reading sports writers to boo the Phillies."

"The fans ought to give the Phillies at least one big crowd this year."[7]

The solution was simple: People would start believing that the Phillies were good as soon as they started winning games. So, they should just do that.

But the Phillies wouldn't have a winning record for another eight years, in 1949. Then they'd go to the World Series and lose in 1950 before not making any kind of postseason appearance again for over 25 years.

Victory is often so close, sometimes only a mere 111 losses out of reach. But baseball remains, the people remain, and the hope remains: the hope for, if not tomorrow or next year, then for that wonderful "*someday*" when fans can finally, *finally* bite into a hot dog and taste something other than shame.

After another eye-rolling summer in 1941, Phillies fans were once again ready to see their local nine bounce back.

"Produce a winning team and the crowds will come out," one fan said of the Phillies' fortunes in 1942. "Everybody loves a winner."

They lost 109 games.

Acknowledgements

The 1941 Phillies played out their season occasionally hating baseball or each other. As they lost 111 games, they likely reached a point at which they were just trying to get through the summer so that it could be over and never talked about again. At no point could they have considered that—nor conceived a reason why—some sneering baseball writer from the future would be looking back on them and sarcastically judging everything they did and said.

There are plenty of other "forgotten teams" to dig up and disgrace 85 years after the fact. But these stories, and the countless others I have written over the years, wouldn't be possible, nor would the way I love to tell them, without the intense coverage and cantankerous editorializing of local newspaper coverage going back a hundred years. It is an aspect of media undervalued by algorithms and inimitable by AI, and without it, we lose so easily the details that flesh out history: What color the sky was the day of an awful loss, where a fight in the stands broke out in the 19th inning, how many dead relatives a reporter claimed to have been visited by while covering a game in the frigid cold. It all gives us curious parties here in the future a bit more context, nuance, and color of moments from which all participants are long dead. Local news coverage opens windows to the past even wider, if you're willing to look through it. And as idiotic people work hard to change what history even was, the truth can be more easily lost.

I must acknowledge the work of my editors at Baseball Prospectus, Craig Goldstein, Patrick Dubuque, and Ginny Searle, and others, all of whom have made my writing better over the years, as well my longtime partners John Stolnis and Liz Roscher, who read this book and offered insightful feedback and advice. The same goes for Matt Albertson, co-chair of Philadelphia's SABR chapter, who I asked to read this manuscript and account for any gross historical inaccuracies. I did that so if there are any, you can blame him instead of me.

I also thank the editors and staff at Brookline Books who accepted this idea for a book, didn't blink as I filled it with annoying prose, and helped make it better with their notes. I also must thank the overseers of the Leslie Jones Collection at the Boston Public Library for supplying some of the images in this book, in addition to SABR for allowing me to include several others. And thank you to my friends at WHYY in Philadelphia, who gave myself, John, and Liz an opportunity several years ago that has resulted in a gratifying partnership.

And to my friends and family who have applauded every rung of the ladder I've managed to climb in sports writing since getting laid off from the only full-time work in the industry I ever had: My grandma and grandpa for taking me on my first baseball road trip, my mom and dad for being wonderful, loving parents and my sisters for always being excited with and for me. And my love, my soulmate, and my wife Aviva for all of her help, support, and willingness to go to baseball games that she hates.

Lastly, to all of the people who've shown up at tailgate after tailgate, listened to podcast after podcast, and demanded to pre-order this book the second I announced its publication, especially the ones who don't even like baseball and still said they were more than happy to buy a book they had no intention of ever reading. Your money's still good.

Time passes quickly and constantly. Thank you for spending some of yours with me and the 1941 Phillies.

Endnotes

Preface

1. H. I. Philips, "The Hot Dog Now Putting on the Dog," *The Roanoke Times*, February 5, 1939, p. 8.
2 Robert W. Maxwell, "Youngsters on Phils are making good and win 5 out of 8 games," *Evening Public Ledger* (Philadelphia, PA), August 2, 1921, p. 16.
3 "Phillies' Poor Showing Also Hurts Athletics," *Camden Courier-Post*, July 16, 1941, p. 14.
4 Ibid.

Prologue: October 1, 1939

1. Whitney Martin, Associated Press (hereafter AP), "Phils Neglected in Fan Forecast," *Clarion-Ledger* (Jackson, MS), April 8, 1939, p. 7.
2. Kirby Higbe and Martin Peter Quigley, *The High Hard One* (University of Nebraska Press, 1967), p. 50.
3. Well, he *could* blame him. And likely did. But Letchas was at least not directly responsible for those things, even if he'd been responsible for the event that allowed them to happen.
4. The Phillies would, eventually, trade Higbe to Brooklyn in November 1940 in exchange for three players and $100,000. He would go on to be an enthusiastic resistor to Jackie Robinson joining the team.
5. The A's, however, won two straight World Series in 1929 and 1930 and won another pennant in 1931. In the nine seasons between 1925 and 1933, the A's hadn't finished lower than third.
6. Fortunately for Kirby Higbe, he'd been traded to Brooklyn by then. "An escapee from the dark recesses of the Phillies' cellar," the Sports Editor for the Associated Press called him, as though the Phillies were a serial killer. Which of course they were. Except they were even worse—their killings were every night, all summer. Their victim? A national pastime.

Characters

1. "Grandstand Crash Kills 1, Injures 25," *Daily News*, May 15, 1927, p. 208.
2. "Phillies Cleared in Death of Man," *Philadelphia Inquirer*, May 28, 1927, p. 20.
3. Whitney Martin, "Sports Trail," *The Tribune*, January 9, 1941, p. 15.
4. Bill Kinney, "Along the Sport Trail," *Rock Island Argus*, June 5, 1941, p. 27.
5. It was a place where people gambled on horse races. I am disappointed to inform you that no horses were there to gamble (at the time of the raid).
6. "Otto Knabe Seized in Gambling Raid," *Philadelphia Inquirer*, March 30, 1941, p. 23.
7. "Dykes Leaves Soon for 21st Camp Trip," *Philadelphia Inquirer*, January 20, 1941, p. 21.
8. United Press (hereafter UP), "Head of Phils' Farm System Will Resign," *Berwick Enterprise*, January 25, 1941, p. 6.
9. "From the Sidelines: Diamond Dust," *The Plain Speaker*, May 21, 1941, p. 14.
10. "The Scoreboard," *Mount Carmel Item*, March 14, 1941, p. 8.
11. "AMEDD Corps History, U.S. Army Dental Corps, United States Army Dental Service in World War II," George E. Armstrong, AMEDD Center of History & Heritage," accessed May 4, 2023, https://achh.army.mil/history/corps-dental-wwii-foreward-wwii.
12. "'Doc' Prothro of Portland Team and His War Club Join the Reds," *Spokane Chronicle*, August 25, 1926, p. 12; "Doc Prothro," Bill Nowlin, Society for American Baseball Research, accessed May 4, 2023, https://sabr.org/bioproj/person/doc-prothro/.
13. "Shortest Arms," *Honolulu Advertiser*, September 24, 1926, p. 10.
14. Whitney Martin, AP, "Doc Prothro Responsible for Phillies' Surprises," *Tampa Bay Times*, May 15, 1939, p. 10.
15. Stan Baumgartner, "Kelly Praises Phil Pitcher; Simmons and Chapman Sign," *Philadelphia Inquirer*, January 16, 1941, p. 28.
16. George Kirksey, UP, "19 Rookies Report for Spring Drills with Doc Prothro," *The Buffalo News*, January 18, 1941, p. 8.
17. "Phils' Group Leaves Today," *Philadelphia Inquirer*, February 28, 1941, p. 32.
18. "War Clauses Mark Baseball Contracts," *Philadelphia Inquirer*, January 3, 1941, p. 22.
19. "Prothro Would Like to be Around," *The Birmingham News*, January 15, 1941, p. 16.
20. Whitney Martin, Special News Service, "Down the Sports Trail," *Pensacola News Journal*, March 30, 1941, p. 10.
21. "Out of Hospital," *The Montreal Star*, March 31, 1941, p. 33.
22. "Doc Prothro," Bill Nowlin, Society for American Baseball Research, accessed May 4, 2023, https://sabr.org/bioproj/person/doc-prothro/.
23. "It's That Kentucky Water," *Detroit Evening Times*, January 5, 1941, p. 16.
24. Stan Baumgartner, "Etten Intends to Hold Job with Phils," *Philadelphia Inquirer*, January 18, 1941, p. 24.

25. Dick Cresap, AP, "Phillies Young Pitching Star is 'No Thrower,'" *The Daily News Journal*, May 16, 1941, p. 4.
26. "Phillies' Tom the Third Looms as Greatest of Hugheses," *Altoona Tribune*, June 27, 1941, p. 17.
27. "Hanover Pitcher Looms Richest Sale in Years," *Wilkes-Barre Times Leader*, August 21, 1940, p. 16.
28. AP, "And They All Play Baseball," *The Shreveport Journal*, July 10, 1941, p. 15.
29. AP, "Phils' Big Need is Power Hitter," *The Express*, February 3, 1940, p. 9.
30. "Hurler Taken on Suggestion of Nig Bragan," *Pensacola News Journal*, March 12, 1940, p. 2.
31. "Sports Slant," Frank Perciola, *Pensacola News Journal*, January 26, 1941, p. 12.
32. "From the Sidelines," *The Plain Speaker*, June 11, 1941, p. 14.
33. "Dan Litwhiler, Phillies Rookie Star, Visits Here," *The Morning Call*, January 6, 1941, p. 14.
34. AP, "Danny Litwhiler's Arm is Alright," *Standard-Speaker*, January 10, 1941, p. 19.
35. "Student," *Daily News*, March 3, 1941, p. 40.
35. Eddie Murphy, "Oaks Face Padres, Seek 10 in a Row," *Oakland Tribune*, July 23, 1937, p. 25.
37. Art Cohn, "Cohn-ing Tower: May Did NOT Tie League Record!" *Oakland Tribune*, July 23, 1937, p. 25.
38. Marc T. McNeil, "Casual Close-ups," *Montreal Gazette*, May 17, 1938, p. 12.
39. W. F. Fox, Jr., "The Yarnin' Basket," *The Indianapolis News*, July 20, 1938, p. 4.
40. "Breaking Up Another Team," *Baltimore Sun*, August 29, 1938, p. 20.
41. James C. Isaminger, "Macks and Phillies Get Seven Players in Draft," *Philadelphia Inquirer*, October 5, 1938, p. 23.
42. "Request Weil to Pitch Johnson in Exhibition Game," *Rock Island Argus*, July 25, 1933, p. 14.
43. "Rookie With Good Strikeout Record Is Signed for Tryout With Rock Island Ball Club," *Rock Island Argus*, March 7, 1928, p. 20.
44. Pat Patten, "The Sport Spotlight," *The Dispatch* (Moline, IL), September 24, 1929, p. 18.
45. "Johnson Pitches Islanders to 5-0 Victory at Marshalltown," Special to the *Rock Island Argus*, August 3, 1928, p. 27.
46. "Si Johnson," Matthew Clifford, Society for American Baseball Research, accessed July 18, 2023, https://sabr.org/bioproj/person/Si-Johnson/.
47. Maurice Corken, "'Rock Island Will Quit Valley Baseball League,' Officials Say," *Rock Island Argus*, November 28, 1931, p. 16.
48. Maurice Corken, "Bottomley's Homer with Bags Loaded Beats Islanders, 7-4," *The Rock Island Argus*, August 1, 1933, p. 14.
49. "Shortstop Sharein Signed for Phillies," *Courier-Post*, February 12, 1940, p. 16.
50. "Derringer of Walters Might Pitch," *Miami Herald*, March 20, 1944, p. 17.

51. Stan Baumgartner, "Prothro to Count Upon Johnson," *Philadelphia Inquirer*, March 4, 1939, p. 23.
52. AP, "Silas Johnson in Top Form," *Evening Star* (Washington, D.C.), April 9, 1941, p. 41.
53. C. J. Doyle, "The Rise of Rizzo: Romance of a Rookie Who made Good From the Start," *Pittsburgh Sun-Telegraph*, April 26, 1938, p. 21.
54. "Boom-Boom Beck," Paul E. Doutrich, Society for American Baseball Research, accessed May 16, 2023, https://sabr.org/bioproj/person/boom-boom-beck/.
55. Jack Koffman, "Podgajny Impressive in Beating Glovers," *The Evening Citizen*, July 23, 1940, p. 10.
56. "The Scoreboard," *Mount Carmel Item*, March 14, 1941, p. 8.

May 15

1. "Phillies Rally in Ninth and Beat Reds, 5-4," *Philadelphia Inquirer*, May 16, 1941, p. 33.
2. Dick Cresap, AP, "Mr. Livingstone, You May Presume, Will Stick in the Major Leagues," *Cumberland Evening Times*, May 16, 1941, p. 21.
3. A snide little remark by the bitter writers of the *Cincinnati Enquirer*, which also repeatedly referred to the Phillies as "coal-holers" on its pages.
4. "Tickled," in this case, meaning "pleased as punch" or "happy as a sandboy." Frey was gleeful at the development as he went from the Cubs, who would finish first in 1938 with an airtight roster, to the Reds, who would finish fourth, but offer far more job opportunities.
5. This is the most annoying kind of hit an opposing team can use to cut into your lead; a floating line drive that just sails over the infield and plops on the grass like a boot tossed in a pond. It's up there with a ground ball some nine-hole hitter accidentally shoots into the outfield. Totally legal in either case, but just … annoying.
6. Bruce Nash and Alan Zullo, *Baseball Hall of Shame 4* (Simon & Schuster, 1991), pp. 11–12.
7. Dick McCann, "Yanks Lose 5th in Row as Chisox Romp, 13-1," *New York Daily News*, May 16, 1941, p. 50.
8. "As DiMaggio Goes," *The Evening News* (Harrisburg, PA), May 29, 1941, p. 13.

May 16–17

1. AP, "British Rout Nazi Forces in West Egypt, As Planes Attack Airports in Syria," *The Wilmington Morning Star*, May 17, 1941, p. 1; AP, "Germans Prepare to Deliver Blow," *The Wilmington Morning Star*, May 17, 1941, p. 1; AP, "F.R. Hints Navy's Use in Red Sea," *The Wilmington Morning Star*, May 17, 1941, p. 1.
2. AP, "Yanks Beat Sox, End Red Streak," *The Wilmington Morning Star*, May 17, 1941, p. 6.

3. W. N. Cox, "Breaks of the Game," *The Virginian-Pilot*, May 17, 1941, p. 10.
4. "Major Shakeup Looms for Reds," Special to the *Philadelphia Inquirer*, May 17, 1941, p. 19.
5. Chic Feldman, "Hatchin' 'Em Out," *The Tribune* (Scranton, PA), May 19, 1941, p. 12.
6. "Yankees Defeat Mackmen, 10-5," Special to the *Philadelphia Inquirer*, July 6, 1941, p. 27.
7. Cy Peterman, "Elaborate Ceremonies Honor A's Pilot; George M. Cohan Sings New Baseball Song," *Philadelphia Inquirer*, May 18, 1941, p. 43.
8. Dick Cresap, AP Feature Service, "Try to Fan Every Man? Not Hughes," *Daily Item*, May 27, 1941, p. 18.

May 18

1. "Walker Cooper," C. Paul Rogers III, Society for American Baseball Research, accessed April 12, 2023, https://sabr.org/bioproj/person/walker-cooper/.
2. Somebody had beef with the Cooper boys. About a month into Walker's recovery, the Cardinals found a bone chip "the size of a lima bean" in Morton's arm.
3. "Cardinals, Phils Trade Brewing," Special to the *Philadelphia Inquirer*, May 20, 1941, p. 27.
4. "Lee Grissom," Charles F. Faber, Society for American Baseball Research, accessed January 27, 2025, https://sabr.org/bioproj/person/lee-grissom/; Harry Grayson, NEA Service, "Phillies Aren't Headed Anywhere in Particular but They'll Have Someone to Sell in Due Time," *Mount Carmel Item*, March 7, 1941, p. 7.

May 19–20

1. George Kirksey, "Yankees Win One from the Browns," *York Daily News-Times*, May 19, 1941, p. 2.
2. Cy Peterman, "Big Sag in Attendance Spurs Late Night Drive," *Philadelphia Inquirer*, May 20, 1941, p. 27.
3. "Phils Score Two in Eleventh to Defeat St. Louis, 6-4," Special to the *Philadelphia Inquirer*, May 21, 1941, p. 31.

May 21

1. "Joe Shortens Grip on Bat to Cure Slump," *The Rock Island Argus*, May 22, 1941, p. 29.
2. International News Service, "Heroes and Goats," *Bradford Evening Star* and *Braford Daily Record*, May 22, 1941, p. 14.
3. AP, "From Lasalle," *The Plain Speaker* (Hazleton, PA), June 27, 1941, p. 20.
4. Edward Burns, "Bill Nicholson Hits No. 8 with Three on Base," *Chicago Tribune*, May 22, 1941, p. 23.

May 22–24

1. Harry Grayson, NEA Service, "Phillies Aren't Headed Anywhere in Particular but They'll Have Someone to Sell in Due Time," *Mount Carmel Item*, March 7, 1941, p. 7.
2. Tommy Holmes, "Silver Lining Dep't: Five with Phillies," *Brooklyn Eagle*, May 23, 1941, p. 15.
3. Hy Turkin, "Phil Pills Prescribed for Dodger Slump," *New York Daily News*, May 24, 1941, p. 28.
4. "2,000 Flock Fans to See Philly Game," *Brooklyn Eagle*, May 23, 1941, p. 15.
5. Rich Westcott, *Tales from the Phillies Dugout* (Sports Publishing, 2006), p. 3.
6. Larry Shenk and Larry Andersen, *Fightin' Phillies: 100 Years of Philadelphia Baseball from the Whiz Kids to the Misfits* (Triumph Books, 2016).
7. "Jack Clements, Old Phil Catcher, Dies in 76th Year," *Philadelphia Inquirer*, May 24, 1941, p. 25.
8. "Get Back!" *New York Daily News*, May 23, 1941, p. 60.

May 25–28

1. Jimmy Wood, "Sportopics," *Brooklyn Eagle*, May 26, 1941, p. 13.
2. Ibid.
3. Ibid.
4. AP, "Pete Reiser Joins Reese as Casualty," *Star Gazette* (Elmira, NY), April 11, 1941, p. 25.
5. Tommy Holmes, "Heroics Cut No Ice with Pete Reiser," *Brooklyn Eagle*, May 26, 1941, p. 13.
6. Hy Turkin, "Reiser Beaned, Saved by Helmet, Dodgers Blank Phillies, 4-0," *Daily News*, April 24, 1941, p. 64.
7. Tommy Holmes, "Heroics Cut No Ice with Pete Reiser," *Brooklyn Eagle*, May 26, 1941, p. 13.
8. Stan Baumgartner, "Dodgers Beat Phils Again," *Philadelphia Inquirer*, May 28, 1941, p. 33.
9. Stan Baumgartner, "Higbe and Durocher at Odds," *The Philadelphia Inquirer*, May 30, 1941, p. 19.
10. "Valley Fans Plan Tribute for Two in Major Leagues," *The Times Leader*, May 24, 1941, p. 13.
11. "Dodgers Nip Phils in 12th Inning, 6-5," *Camden Courier-Post*, May 29, 1941, p. 18.
12. Hy Turkin, "Reiser's hit Defeats Phils, 6-5, in 12th," *Brooklyn Eagle*, May 29, 1941, p. 36.
13. Jack Smith, "Nats' Protest Yanks' 10-8 Victory; DiMag Homers," *New York Daily News*, May 28, 1941, p. B54.

14. George M. Mawhinney, "Throng Roars for U.S. Aid to Defeat Axis," *Philadelphia Inquirer*, May 29, 1941, p. 1.
15. John M. Cummings, "German Song Out of Place," *Philadelphia Inquirer*, May 29, 1941, p. 4.

May 29

1. Jimmy Wood, "Sportopics," *Brookyln Daily Eagle*, May 29, 1941, p. 11.
2. Tommy Holmes, "Dodgers Must Brace to Beat Giants, Cards," *Brooklyn Eagle*, May 29, 1941, p. 11.
3. "Bruner of Phils Gets Army Call," *The Philadelphia Inquirer*, May 30, 1941, p. 19.

June 1–3

1. Richard Ben Cramer, *Joe DiMaggio: The Hero's Life* (Touchstone Books, 2001), p. 22.
2. Bert Nakaji, "Covering the Sports Dirt with Bert," *Hawaii Tribune-Herald*, June 1, 1941, p. 7.
3. "Touching the Sacks," *Scrantonian Tribune*, June 1, 1941, p. 28.
4. UP, "Pope Offers Basis for Lasting Peace; Seeks a World Free of Want, Regimentation," *Philadelphia Inquirer*, June 2, 1941, p. 1.
5. "Bobby Bragan," Maurice Bouchard and David Fleitz, Society for American Baseball Research, accessed April 22, 2023, https://sabr.org/bioproj/person/bobby-bragan/.
6. They probably did not do this. They had been on base before. They were professional baseball players, after all. Just not professional ballplayers very familiar with success.
7. Jane Leslie Kift, "Peonies Gain Favor for Blooming Qualities," *Philadelphia Inquirer*, June 1, 1941, p. 62.
8. Stan Baumgartner, "Phils Lose Pair to Cubs; Bragan Hits 4-Run Homer," *Philadelphia Inquirer*, June 2, 1941, p. 25.
9. Grissom appeared in one game for Brooklyn before being traded to the Phillies in May 1941. The Phillies would lose all but three of the 32 games in which he'd appear, and win only one of 23 between May 13 and August 13.
10. Stan Baumgartner, "Litwhiler's Homers Aid Phils; Rain Halts A's; Sox Play Today," *Philadelphia Inquirer*, June 3, 1941, p. 23.
11. Edward Burns, "Phils' Two Kids Beat Cubs and French, 3-2," *Chicago Tribune*, June 3, 1941, p. 21.
12. "Phils Lose Services of Marty to Grip," *Evening Courier*, June 4, 1941, p. 22.
13. "Hughes Hurls One-Hitter as Phillies Triumph Over Cubs, 7-0," *The Morning Post* (Camden, NJ), June 4, 1941, p. 18.
14. Pat Robinson, International News Service (hereafter INS), "Hughes, Carpenter are Top Recruits," *Lexington Herald-Leader*, June 4, 1941, p. 8.

15. "Phils, Reds to Try Again Under Arc Lights Tonight," *Camden Courier-Post*, June 5, 1941, p. 18.
16. George Kirksey, UP, "Lou Gehrig, Good Boy of Baseball, is Dead," *The News-Herald*, June 3, 1941, p. 9.
17. UP, "'Iron Man,' Lou Gehrig, 37, Former Yankees Star, Dies," *Muskogee Daily Phoenix and Times-Democrat*, June 3, 1941, p. 6.
18. AP, "Harridge Leads Baseball World in Tribute to Gehrig," *Philadelphia Inquirer*, June 3, 1941, p. 24.
19. AP, "Yankees Stunned by News of Death," *Atlanta Constitution*, June 3, 1941, p. 19.
20. Ted Williams and John Underwood, *My Turn at Bat: The Story of My Life* (Simon & Schuster, 1969, 1988), p. 60.

June 6

1. "Johnny Vander Meer," James W. Johnson, Society for American Baseball Research, accessed May 3, 2023, https://sabr.org/bioproj/person/johnny-vander-meer/.
2. INS, "Reds Will Try 'Conclusions' With Phillies," *Lexington Herald-Leader*, June 4, 1941, p. 8.
3. Stan Baumgartner, "Dan Litwhiler Ruins No-Hitter," *Philadelphia Inquirer*, June 7, 1941, p. 19.
4. For the Tulsa Oilers in the Texas League.

June 7–9

1. "Hitler is Challenged in Launching of Minelayer Terror Here," *Philadelphia Inquirer*, June 7, 1941, p. 6.
2. "Size of Hamburgers Starts Store Brawl," *Philadelphia Inquirer*, June 8, 1941, p. 29; "Rubbish Removed in South Oak Lane," *Philadelphia Inquirer*, June 8, 1941, p. 29; "Battleship South Dakota is Launched at Camden Yard," *Philadelphia Inquirer*, June 8, 1941, p. 29.
3. AP, "Slump Over, They Cheer Litwhiler," *Pottsville Republican*, June 5, 1941, p. 18.
4. Stan Baumgartner, "Blanton Blanks Bucs for Phils," *Philadelphia Inquirer*, June 8, 1941, p. 40.
5. "Then There's the Comeback of Cy Blanton," *Pittsburgh Sun-Telegraph*, June 9, 1941, p. 18.
6. Ibid.
7. Stan Baumgartner, "Phils Defeat Pittsburgh, 5-2, After Losing Opener, 12-2," *Philadelphia Inquirer*, June 9, 1941, p. 22.
8. Stan Baumgartner, "Macks Beaten, 7-5, in Bill; Quakers Fall, 12-2, Win 2d, 5-2," *Philadelphia Inquirer*, June 9, 1941, p. 19.
9. Edward F. Balinger, "Bucs Beat Phils, 12 to 2, Then Lose Second, 5 to 2," *Pittsburgh Post-Gazette*, June 9, 1941, p. 14.

10. "Illness Hits Phils; Rizzo, Marty Out," *The Daily Advocate*, June 6, 1941, p. 6.
11. "May 30, 1939: Johnny Rizzo Sets Pirates Record with Nine RBI in a Game," Bob LeMoine, Society for American Baseball Research, accessed June 5, 2023, https://sabr.org/gamesproj/game/may-30-1939-johnny-rizzo-sets-pirates-record-with-nine-rbis-in-a-game/.
12. Stan Baumgartner, "Phils Defeat Pittsburg, 5-2, After Losing Opener, 12-2," *Philadelphia Inquirer*, June 6, 1941, p. 22.
13. Stan Baumgartner, "Phils Blanked by Bucs, 5-0," *Philadelphia Inquirer*, June 10, 1941, p. 25.
14. Harry Grayson, "Practice Makes Batters Great," *The Bangor Daily News*, June 9, 1941, p. 15.

June 10–11

1. Joe Trimble, "Athletics Hand Bobo 1st Loss as Yankee, 5-3," *New York Daily News*, August 7, 1947, p. 67.
2. UP, "Fan Hurriedly Removes Pants at Shibe Park," *El Paso Times*, August 26, 1938, p. 10.
3. Stan Baumgartner, "Warneke Checks Phils with 1 Hit," *Philadelphia Inquirer*, June 11, 1941, p. 30.
4. "Lon Warneke," Don Duren, Society for American Baseball Research, accessed May 7, 2023, https://sabr.org/bioproj/person/lon-warneke/.
5. Ibid.
6. Bruce Nash and Alan Zullo, *Baseball Hall of Shame 4* (Simon & Schuster, 1991), p. 31.
7. Stan Baumgartner, "Cards Top Quakers in 10 Innings, 3-2," *Philadelphia Inquirer*, June 12, 1941, p. 29.
8. Paul Menton, "Discussion Starts on All-Star Teams," *Baltimore Sun*, June 11, 1941, p. 23.
9. Jack Smith, "Henrich Borrowed DiMag's Bat and Started Hitting," *New York Daily News*, June 12, 1941, p. 60.
10. Jimmy Powers, "The Power House," *New York Daily News*, June 12, 1941, p. 60.
11. "Phils Acquire Giant," *Press and Sun-Bulletin*, June 12, 1941, p. 30.
12. George Kirksey, UP, "Bat Streak of DiMaggio Stirs Fans," *Democrat and Chronicle*, July 8, 1941, p. 20.
13. Paul Scheffels, "Harman Amazes Fans," *The Brooklyn Citizen*, July 9, 1941, p. 7.
14. AP, "Phils Bombard 44th Div., 15-0," *New York Daily News*, July 10, 1941, p. 49.

June 14–16

1. AP, "Sports Roundup," *The York Dispatch*, July 7, 1941, p. 11.
2. "Baseball," *Cincinnati Enquirer*, June 14, 1941, p. 36.
3. Matt Zabitka, "Podgajny Nixed Scout Offers After Sour Predictions About Stan Musial, Bob Lemon," *Delaware County Times*, June 4, 1953, p. 39; Podgajny would

go on to become a baseball scout who claimed that Stan Musial would never hit, and that his rookie season, in which Musial had hit .426, had been all luck. He also said Bob Lemon couldn't pitch. Both are in the Hall of Fame. Eventually Podgajny would get into automobile sales.

4. AP Feature Service, "These Pitchers Almost Had No-Hitters," *Lexington Herald*, June 15, 1941, p. 11.
5. Cy Peterman, "Expect 50,000 to See Louis Fight Conn; Bomber 4-1 Choice for New York Battle," *Philadelphia Inquirer*, June 18, 1941, p. 33.
6. Sid Feder, "Joe Louis 2-5 To Beat Conn," *Philadelphia Inquirer*, June 17, 1941, p. 21.

June 17–19

1. "Jimmy Smith," Jim Sandoval, Society for American Baseball Research, accessed May 8, 2023, https://sabr.org/bioproj/person/jimmy-smith/.
2. "She Plays Juliet to Conn's Romeo," *Philadelphia Inquirer*, June 18, 1941, p. 33.
3. "St. Louis Drubs Phillies, 7 to 3," Special to the *Philadelphia Inquirer*, June 19, 1941, p. 26.
4. John Webster, "Foe's Mistake Gives Joe Deciding Break," *Philadelphia Inquirer*, June 19, 1941, p. 23.
5. "Cards Beat Phils in Eleventh, 7-6," Special to the *Philadelphia Inquirer*, June 20, 1941, p. 27.
6. "Cardinals Hand Unhappy Phillies 40th Defeat of the Season," *St. Louis Post-Dispatch*, June 20, 1941, p. 2B.
7. W. Vernon Tietjen, "Johnny Mize, Back in Lineup, Helps Cards Defeat Phils, 7-6," *St. Louis Star-Times*, June 20, 1941, p. 18.
8. "Lines on the News," Bob French, *Philadelphia Inquirer*, June 19, 1941, p. 25.
9. AP, "Yanks Spill White Sox, 7-2," *Philadelphia Inquirer*, June 20, 1941, p. 28.
10. AP, "Yanks Trip White Sox in Third of Set, 7-2," *The Commercial Appeal*, June 20, 1941, p. 20.

June 20–22

1. *The Marine Recruiter*, December 1942, p. 8.
2. "Frankie Gustine," Gregory H. Wolf, Society for American Baseball Research, accessed May 10, 2023, https://sabr.org/bioproj/person/frankie-gustine/.
3. Jack Mahon, "MacPhail Wants Leiber or Rizzo in Walker Deal," *The Times-Tribune*, June 11, 1941, p. 19.
4. "Big Bats," Jack Ryder, *Cincinnati Enquirer*, August 25, 1935, p. 26.
5. "Crouch is Sold to Cardinals," *Philadelphia Inquirer*, June 22, 1941, p. 35.
6. Dick Cresap, AP, "Danny Litwhiler Confident He'll Match Temperature Rise," *The Evening Review* (Liverpool, OH), June 23, 1941, p. 11.
7. AP, "N.Y. Area Big League Teams Going to Town," *The Plain Speaker* (Hazleton, PA), June 23, 1941, p. 12.

8. Stan Baumgartner, "Phil Hurlers Put More Zip on Ball," *Philadelphia Inquirer*, March 5, 1940, p. 26.
9. AP, "Draft Gets Roy Bruner," *Harrisburg Telegraph*, May 20, 1941, p. 11.

June 24–26

1. Lou Smith, "Bucky Walters Breezes to Victory Over Lowly Phils, 5-1," *Cincinnati Enquirer*, June 25, 1941, p. 13.
2. "Sports-o-grams," *Mount Carmel Item*, June 26, 1941, p. 8.
3. AP Feature, "Phillies' Find," *The Daily Item* (Lynn, MA), June 26, 1941, p. 16.
4. AP, "Red Edge Up on Giants by Winning Pair from Phutile Phils," *Dayton Daily News*, June 26, 1941, p. 15.
5. Ibid.
6. "Danny Litwhiler at Mother's Bedside," *Philadelphia Inquirer*, June 27, 1941, p. 25; AP, "Mother of Hans Lobert, Phillies coach, dies," *Altoona Tribune*, June 27, 1941, p. 16.
7. "Batter in Slump Should Point Toe Toward Pitcher, Says Joe," *The Binghamton Press*, June 25, 1941, p. 16.
8. Ibid.
9. AP, "Hitting Streak is Not Worrying Joe DiMaggio," *Poughkeepsie Eagle-News*, June 27, 1941, p. 16.
10. Harry Ferguson, UP, "Joe DiMaggio Placed Seven Times on Nine," *The Columbus Telegram* (Columbus, NE), June 25, 1941, p. 6.
11. "Batter in Slump Should Point Toe Toward Pitcher, Says Joe," *The Binghamton Press*, June 25, 1941, p. 16.

June 27–29

1. "Spin on Himself," *The Winnipeg Tribune*, June 28, 1941, p. 21.
2. Joe Trimble, "Giants Win; Etten Hurt," *New York Daily News*, June 28, 1941, p. 29.
3. AP, "Phils Lose," *Press of Atlantic City*, June 28, 1941, p. 12.
4. Dick McCann, "Phillies Trim Giants, 3-2, in 12-Inning Battle," *New York Daily News*, June 29, 1941, p. 33C.
5. AP, "Gerry Nugent Indicates Shake-Up for Phillies," *The Times Leader*, June 28, 1941, p. 15.
6. "Homers Will Give Joe Edge if He Ties Sisler's Record," *Brooklyn Eagle*, June 28, 1941, p. 9.
7. Len Unger, "Yanks Look Good," *Republican and Herald*, June 28, 1941, p. 9.
8. "Phils Defeat Giants in 12th," Special to the *Philadelphia Inquirer*, June 29, 1941, p. 29.
9. "Phils Defeat Giants in 12th," Special to the *Philadelphia Inquirer*, June 29, 1941, p. 29.
10. AP, "The Umps, Bless 'Um, Are Saved," *Argus-Leader* (Sioux Falls, ND), July 22, 1941, p. 8.

11. Harold Claasen, "Sisler the Best Ever, Says Collins," *The Daily News Leader*, July 10, 1941, p. 8.
12. AP, "DiMaggio Aims at his Minor League Mark of 61," *Fort Worth Star-Telegram*, July 12, 1941, p. 3.
13. "Giants Rap Four Phillie Hurlers to Triumph, 10-7," Special to the *Philadelphia Inquirer*, June 30, 1941, p. 17.
14. "Giants Get Break from Schedule," Special to the *Brooklyn Eagle*, June 30, 1941, p. 13.
15. "Ace Adams," Warren Corbett, Society for American Baseball Research, accessed November 11, 2024, https://sabr.org/bioproj/person/ace-adams/.
16. Gordon Graham, "Graham Crackers," *Journal and Courier*, June 30, 1941, p. 12.
17. Norman L. Macht, *The Grand Old Man of Baseball: Connie Mack in His Final Years, 1932–1956* (University of Nebraska Press, 2015).
18. Rich Marazzi and Len Fiorito, *Baseball Players of the 1950s: A Biographical Dictionary of all 1,560 Major Leaguers* (McFarland & Company, 2009), pp. 252–53.

June 30–July 2

1. Hy Turkin, "Flock Rips Phils, 9-2; Tie for 1st," *New York Daily News*, July 1, 1941, p. 50.
2. Hy Turkin, "Owen Beaned, Out Five Days," *New York Daily News*, July 1, 1941, p. 50.
3. Cy Peterman, "Strictly Sports: In Hailing DiMag's Feat Just Don't Forget Sisler," *Philadelphia Inquirer*, July 2, 1941, p. 29.
4. "Phils Knock Brooklyn Into 2d Place, 6-4, as St. Louis Turns Back Pittsburgh, 11 to 7," Special to the *Philadelphia Inquirer*, July 2, 1941, p. 29.
5. Cy Peterman, "Phils Sabotaging Selves, But It's Not Intentional," *Philadelphia Inquirer*, July 14, 1941, p. 19.
6. "Phils Got a Prize," *Republican and Herald* (Pottsville, PA), July 2, 1941, p. 10.
7. "May Ambidextrous," *The Evening News* (Harrisburg, PA), July 2, 1941, p. 190.
8. Bob French, "Lines on the News," *Philadelphia Inquirer*, July 3, 1941, p. 23.

July 3–5

1. "The Daily Limerick," *Philadelphia Inquirer*, July 5, 1941, p. 1.
2. INS, "DiMaggio's Bat to be Auctioned Off," *Democrat and Chronicle*, July 5, 1941, p. 19.
3. Glenn Jordan, "Sea Dogs' first female coach already having an impact on Red Sox prospects," *Portland Press Herald*, May 28, 2022, https://www.pressherald.com/2022/05/28/sea-dogs-first-female-coach-making-a-quick-impact-on-red-sox-prospects/.
4. "Bobby Bragan," Maurice Bouchard and David Fleitz, Society for American Baseball Research, accessed May 18, 2023, https://sabr.org/bioproj/person/bobby-bragan/.

5. "Johnny Podgajny," Gregory H. Wolf, Society for American Baseball Research, accessed March 29, 2023, https://sabr.org/bioproj/person/johnny-podgajny/.
6. "Ryba Faces Sundra and Senators," *Transcript-Telegram* (Holyoke, MA), April 17, 1941, p. 12.
7. "Braves Beat Phils Twice," *Philadelphia Inquirer*, July 5, 1941, p. 15.
8. "Lost and Found," *Philadelphia Inquirer*, July 6, 1941, p. 1.

July 6–9

1. Cy Peterman, "Speak of Dream Games, Here's Senator Nightmare," *Philadelphia Inquirer*, July 8, 1941, p. 21.
2. AP, "Phillies Win At Camp Dix," *The Morning Call* (Allentown, PA), July 10, 1941, p. 17.
3. "Why Dom DiMaggio Gave up Golf," *The Boston Globe*, July 23, 1941, p. 20.
4. Jimmy Powers, "Powerhouse," *Daily News* (New York), July 30, 1941, p. 50.
5. Jeff Lenburg, *Baseball's All Star Game: A Game by Game Guide* (iUniverse.com, Inc., 1986, 2001), pp. 30–31.
6. Ted Williams and John Underwood, *My Turn at Bat: The Story of My Life* (Simon & Schuster, 1969, 1988), p. 74.
7. Ibid., p. 219.
8. Ibid., p. 236.
9. Ibid., p. 135.
10. AP, "Ted Williams is No Longer 'Kid,'" Earl Hilligan, *The Morning Call*, June 9, 1941, p. 15.
11. Ted Williams and John Underwood, *My Turn at Bat: The Story of My Life* (Simon & Schuster, 1969, 1988), pp. 20–21.
12. Al Vermeer, NEA Service, "Freddie Fitzsimmons was Smart—Quiet as Skipper of Phils Before Job Got Him," *The News-Herald* (Franklin, PA), July 6, 1945, p. 8.

July 10–12

1. Wes Stillwell, "One Man's Views," *Millville Daily Republican*, July 10, 1941, p. 6.
2. AP, "Pirates Tab 5 in Eighth to Nip Phils," *The Mercury* (Pottstown, PA), July 11, 1941, p. 16.
3. Joe Gootter, "Sportograms," *The News* (Paterson, NJ), July 29, 1941, p. 15.
4. Harry Grayson, "Grayson's Scoreboard," *The Selma Times-Journal*, July 16, 1941, p. 5.
5. Cy Peterman, "DiMaggio Hitting Streak Might Reach 60 Games," *Philadelphia Inquirer*, July 11, 1941, p. 25.
6. "Sport-o-grams," *Mount Carmel Item*, July 12, 1941, p. 3.
7. Ibid.

July 13–15

1. "Press Box Prattle," *Burlington Daily News*, July 29, 1937, p. 8.
2. "Lefty Hoerst," Gregory H. Wolf, Society for American Baseball Research, accessed July 19, 2023, https://sabr.org/bioproj/person/Lefty-Hoerst/.
3. Stan Baumgartner, "Phils Play Cards Tomorrow; Fans to Honor Frank Hoerst," *Philadelphia Inquirer*, July 12, 1941, p. 16.
4. Among certain demographics, that is. Globally it was a smashing success.
5. Harry Grayson, NEA Service, "DiMaggio's Goal Own Minor Mark of 61; Injury Gave him to Yankees at Bargain Rate; Others Gave Up When He Hurt Knee in Jitney," *Blackwell Journal-Tribune*, July 16, 1941, p. 5.
6. AP, "Plight of Phils Again Discussed," *Arizona Republic*, July 16, 1941, p. 12.
7. Cy Peterman, "Phils Sabotaging Selves, But It's Not Intentional," *Philadelphia Inquirer*, July 14, 1941, p. 19.
8. The first man up with the bags juiced was shortstop Bobby Bragan. He worked a 2-0 count and then, instead of continuing to work it, took a mighty swing at the next pitch and popped out. The Phillies zipped up whatever the opposite of a rally was with a ground ball double play moments later.
9. Stan Baumgartner, "Cards Annex Long Fray, 2-1," *The Philadelphia Inquirer*, July 16, 1941, p. 25.

July 16–17

1. Bill Kinney, "Along the Sport Trail," *Rock Island Argus*, July 17, 1941, p. 24.
2. "Phila. To Stage All-Star Game," *Philadelphia Inquirer*, July 18, 1941, p. 30.
3. "Bob French, Lines on the News," *Philadelphia Inquirer*, July 18, 1941, p. 29.
4. "Imagine My Embarrassment," *Philadelphia Inquirer*, July 17, 1941, p. 15.
5. Stan Baumgartner, "Cubs Rout Phils, Root Wins 298th," *Philadelphia Inquirer*, July 17, 1941, p. 22.
6. Frances Drake, "Horoscopes," *Philadelphia Inquirer*, July 17, 1941, p. 18.
7. Stan Baumgartner, "Rain Checks Phils and Cubs In 2-to-2 Tie," *Philadelphia Inquirer*, July 18, 1941, p. 30.
8. David Jones, *Joe DiMaggio: A Biography* (Greenwood Press, 2004), p. 70.
9. "Baseball," *Cincinnati Enquirer*, August 24, 1941, p. 60.

The Rest of the Season

1. Bill Kinney, "Along the Sports Trail," *Rock Island Argus*, July 17, 1941, p. 24.
2. Judson Bailey, "Prothro Goes Hunting," *The Gazette* (Cedar Rapids, IA), August 17, 1941, p. 12.
3. "Baseball," *Cincinnati Enquirer*, August 24, 1941, p. 60.

4. "Used to Phillies," *Wilkes-Barre Times Leader*, September 6, 1941, p. 11.
5. AP, "Prothro Switch Only Rumor, Officials Claim," *The Daily Item* (Sunbury, PA), August 19, 1941, p. 13.
6. Jack Troy, "Doc's Coming Back," *Atlanta Constitution*, August 21, 1941, p. 19.
7. "Sports' Silliness," *The High Point Enterprise* (High Point, NC), September 7, 1941, p. 17.
8. "Future is Very Dark for Phils," *Harrisburg Sunday Courier*, August 24, 1941, p. 5.
9. AP, "Step Up and Swing, Don't Think," *The Daily Times*, August 9, 1941, p. 14.
10. AP, "Litwhiler's 13th Lift Averts Philly Blackout," *The Tribune*, August 23, 1941, p. 12.
11. Bill Burk, "Sports Shorts," *Delaware County Daily Times*, August 19, 1941, p. 10.
12. "Ruth Hughes, 20, Sister of Pitcher Tommy Hughes, Dies," *The Times-Tribune*, August 20, 1941, p. 12.
13. Eddie Brietz, "Sports Round-Up," *The Plain Speaker*, August 12, 1941, p. 10.
14. "Phils Reported Ready to Sell Ringtown Star," *The Plain Speaker*, August 22, 1941, p. 16.
15. AP, "Yankees DiMaggio at Big Party," *The Ogden Standard-Examiner* (Ogden, UT), August 31, 1941, p. 11.
16. Bob French, "Lines on the News," *Philadelphia Inquirer*, September 6, 1941, p. 35.
17. "Dodger Finale Real Burlesque," *Brooklyn Eagle*, September 29, 1941, p. 13.
18. "Athletics Outdraw Phils at Home by 3 to 1 Margin" *Courier-Post*, July 8, 1941, p. 16.
19. AP, "MacPhail's No. 1 Maneuver Brings Joy to Flatbushers," *Press of Atlantic City*, September 30, 1941, p. 11.
20. Ted Williams and John Underwood, *My Turn at Bat: The Story of My Life* (Simon & Schuster, 1969, 1988), p. 89.
21. David Bloom, "Doc Prothro Unhappy," *The Commercial Appeal* (Memphis, TN), April 2, 1943, p. 16.
22. Ryan Lawrence, "Another Loss That's Not Worth Watching," *Philadelphia Daily News*, July 3, 2014, p. 55.

Epilogue

1. Bill Dooli, "This and That," *Camden Morning Post*, June 1, 1945, p. 26.
2. He slashed .243/.297/.413 for his career in Shibe Park, putting it right around the kind of output you'd expect from Vince DiMaggio. He'd also been named an all-star in each of the last two seasons, despite leading the league in nothing but strikeouts. With the Phillies, he'd lead the league in strikeouts again, for the fourth year in a row.
3. Rich Westcott, *Tales from the Philadelphia Phillies Dugout* (Sports Publishing, 2012), p. 44.

4. "Kelly Asks Frick to Force Phils' Sale," *Camden Morning Post*, September 22, 1941, p. 16.
5. Ted Williams and John Underwood, *My Turn at Bat: The Story of My Life* (Simon & Schuster, 1969, 1988), p. 120.
6. Cy Peterman, "'Fresh Money for Sport Too Often is a Mirage," *Philadelphia Inquirer*, January 2, 1941, p. 21.
7. "Loyal Fans Say Phils Could Lick A's; Macks Dared to Play City Series," *Philadelphia Inquirer*, August 24, 1941, p. 35.

Index